Battleships

WITHDRAWN

Battleships

ANTONY PRESTON

Distributed by
Frederick Fell Publishers Inc.
386 Park Avenue South,
New York, NY 10016.

Published 1982 by
Bison Books Inc.
17 Sherwood Place, Greenwich, CT 06830,
USA.

ISBN 0-8119-0462-8

Printed in Hong Kong

CONTENTS

WOODEN WALLS AND IRONCLADS

No ship has ever achieved the aura of power of the battleship. Other warships have been more powerful, but throughout their short reign battleships were publicly equated with power. In days gone by national strength was reckoned in dreadnoughts and even as late as 1982, long after the battleships has ceased to count as a unit of strength, the US Navy is recommissioning a battleship to provide heavy-gun support.

To understand where it all started we have to go back five centuries to the time when it became feasible to mount heavy guns on board ships. A Frenchman called Descharges is traditionally regarded as the inventor of a method of cutting gunports in the lower deck and fitting them with hinged lids, about 1500. It was not long before a complete tier of guns was possible, and the first English man o'war with a complete lower gundeck appeared sometime after 1515. This transition was also being made in other navies of Europe, away from fighting with land-weapons between opposing groups of *men*. From now on the emphasis would be on damaging the enemy *ship*. Boarding and

hand-to-hand fighting would last for another four centuries but, from the sixteenth century, anti-ship weapons assumed ever more importance.

The following century saw greater discipline in tactics, with the ships fighting in a 'line of battle' to increase the strength of the 'battery' or 'broadside.' The need for more gunpower forced designers to add a second tier of guns, and by the early years of the seventeenth century three-deckers were being built. Gun design was improving, and some of the bewildering nomenclature of the previous century had been weeded out. Cannon

Above: Nelson falls mortally wounded on the deck of the *Victory* at Trafalgar.
Below: HMS *Brunswick* locked in combat with *L'Achille* and *Le Vengeur du Peuple* at the Glorious First of June, 1794.

became known as 42-pounders, demi-canon as 32-pounders, culverins as 18-pounders and demi-culverins as 9-pounders.

During the eighteenth century the steady growth in size and fighting power went on. The 1st Rate of 100 guns was expensive to build and man, and relatively few could be afforded. Thus a much greater number of three-decked 2nd Rates (90 to 98 guns) and two-decked 3rd Rates (64 to 84 guns) made up the balance of the fleet.

The line of development which had started in the early 1500s reached its peak at Trafalgar in 1805, when the main British Fleet under Vice-Admiral Lord Nelson met and destroyed a superior French–Spanish Fleet under Admiral Villeneuve. Nelson had three 100-gun ships, the *Victory*, *Royal Sovereign* and *Britannia* as well as two 98s while Villeneuve had the giant 130-gun *Santisima Trinidad*, the 112-gun *Santa Anna* and *Principe de Asturias* and the 100-gun *Rayo*. But the battle was decided by the 2nd and 3rd Rates, from the 98-gun *Dreadnought* and the 80-gun *Bucentaure* down to the elderly 64-gun *Agamemnon*, *Africa*, *Polyphemus* and *San Leandro*.

This slow majestic progress was interrupted by an innovation that was ultimately to destroy the wooden walls. In 1822 the French artilleryman Henri Paixhans published a treatise on how the French Navy could avenge its recent shattering defeat. He argued that France must find a technological answer, an 'equalizer' which would wipe out the British lead in warships. His solution was merely an adaptation of an old idea; the hollow cast-iron bomb (which had been around since the seventeenth

Above: A French two-deck ship of the line is dismasted during an engagement with the British in 1758.

century) could be redesigned to be fired from the 'long' ship-gun. If such a shell was to lodge in an enemy ship's timbers it would tear an enormous hole and probably start a fire. There was nothing that a contemporary sailor feared as much as fire, for with her mass of tarred cordage and dry timbers a wooden man o' war was likely to become a fiery death-trap.

Paixhans had little trouble in getting his ideas accepted, but instead of a fleet of small steamers with shell guns demolishing the Royal Navy, he had to endure the depressing sight of the British equipping their ships with his shell-gun. The French introduced their *canon-obusier* in 1824 and the British issued their first 8-inch shell guns two years later, but both navies continued to make solid-shot guns for the simple reason that they were more accurate over longer ranges. By the end of the 1830s most three-deckers carried about 60 per cent of the standard type to 40 per cent shell guns. The method of ignition was primitive but effective: the wooden fuze was ignited by the flash of the black powder charge as the gun fired, and a simple time-delay prevented detonation until (it was hoped) the shell struck the target.

The Royal Navy tried to propel a small sloop by steam as early as 1814 and seven years later the first paddle sloops were ordered from the Royal Dockyards. There was no attempt to build a steam powered battleship at this stage for one very simple reason: no new ones were laid down in the years after Waterloo, because so many hulls were already on the stocks. In the late 1820s a new class of 120-gun 1st Rates was begun, whose armament was to be six 68-pdrs and 114 32-pdrs. Even bigger ships followed, for the Royal Navy had a huge investment in wooden shipbuilding.

It was only a matter of time before steam power was installed in a big warship. The paddle wheel was only suited to small warships because it would interfere with too large a percentage of the broadside of guns. As early as May 1840 the Admiralty decided to build a screw steamship, the sloop *Rattler*. In November 1845 work started on converting the incomplete 3rd Rate *Ajax* into a 'screw blockship' and when she went to sea on 23 September 1846 she was the world's first seagoing steam battleship. As

she and her sister *Edinburgh* carried only 58 guns they were theoretically inferior to other two-deckers but it was recognized that they could out-maneuver any sail-powered warship afloat and so they were given the vague designation of 'screw block-ships.'

The pace now accelerated as both the French and British put steam engines into all new ships of the line and converted as many of the existing hulls as they could afford. By 1853, on the eve of the Crimean War, the screw propeller and the shell-gun were firmly established. The small actions of the 1840s had shown that shells were effective but it was not until November 1853, when a Russian squadron of six ships of the line and four smaller ships trapped and sank a Turkish squadron of eleven ships at Sinope, that the major navies took the threat to their ships seriously. What made Sinope important was that all the Turkish ships had been set on fire, and the fact that the British and French, with their large fleets of wooden sailing ships, had just let themselves be drawn into a war with the Russians.

The Anglo-French fleet was to experience the new technology when it tried to support the land attack on Sevastopol with a bombardment of the forts. On 17 October 1854 the lumbering two-deckers and three-deckers went into action, the sailing ships each being towed by a small steamer. After about an hour and a half the *Albion* had been set on fire twice and sustained severe casualties from four shell hits. She was towed out of action stern first, and then it was the turn of the *Queen* to be set on fire by red-hot shot and the frigate *Arethusa* to be knocked about. The French *Ville de Paris* also suffered from a mortar shell under the poop which caused many casualties, but apart from the *Albion* all damaged ships were ready for action next day.

Although the Allies had not suffered heavily they took energetic steps to make sure that the next engagement would be on more favorable terms. The French Navy's *Directeur du Matériel*'s immediate suggestion was to fill the hollow sides of a ship with cannon balls, but the Royal Navy came up with a more sensible idea in 4-inch wrought iron plating. Both countries had experimented with wrought iron warship hulls in the 1840s but had lost interest when it became obvious that iron splintered when struck by solid shot. But by 1854 the science of metallurgy had advanced and wrought iron now had sufficient

elasticity to be able to absorb the energy of a hit without shredding into lethal splinters.

The French and British collaborated on the hurried design of ten 'floating batteries,' with a single gun deck, 4-inch plating on the sides and a simple barque rig and a steam engine to drive them at four knots. They could hardly steam or sail adequately, but they were intended to be towed to their theater of operations. The French ships, called *Congréve*, *Devastation*, *Foudroyant*, *Lavé* and *Tonnant* were ordered shortly after the Sevastopol bombardment and were ready the following summer, and the British *Aetna*, *Glatton*, *Meteor*, *Thunder* and *Trusty* were ready in April 1855. A series of small delays prevented the British floating batteries from getting out to the Black Sea in time for a big assault on the forts at the mouths of the Dnieper and Bug Rivers, and so the honor for the first action fought by armorplated ships goes to the French. On 17 October 1855 the five French batteries opened fire against Kinbourn Kosa, a group of five forts guarding the approaches to Odessa. An hour and a half later the forts surrendered, having seen that the ships were impervious to the rain of red-hot shot and shell. Despite being hit repeatedly the only casualties suffered were from splinters entering through the embrasures or the overhead hatches.

The Crimean War came to an end before the floating batteries could prove themselves in a massive assault on Kronstadt planned for the spring of 1856. With it ended very quickly that brief *entente* between Great Britain and France for almost immediately the government of Napoleon III embarked on a program to expand the Navy. By March 1858 preparations had been completed for building four 'ironclad' battleships and the Press was full of heady speculation about the end of British naval supremacy. The British, with the lessons of Sinope, Sevastopol and Kinbourn very much in mind, looked for some answer to the French threat.

The French were lucky in having the leading naval architect of the day, Dupuy de Lôme. He took the design of his outstanding steam two-decker *Napoleon*, built in 1850, and modified it to carry iron side plating capable of keeping out the newest 16-cm (6.5-in) explosive shell fired by the 50-pdr rifled muzzle loading gun. What resulted was hardly a beautiful ship, for *La Gloire* was squat and ugly, but she was soundly executed and fully justified the fame of being the world's first armored *seagoing*

Above: The British floating battery *Terror* seen just before her launch in 1856, too late for the Crimean War.

battleship. She was to be followed by two sisters, *L'Invincible* and *La Normandie* and a slightly larger ship, *La Couronne*.

For a while the British appeared to be paralyzed by the specter of resurgent French naval power, but behind the scenes there was feverish activity. During the summer of 1858 trials were carried out on test-samples of iron plates fitted to the side of the old ship of the line *Alfred* and two floating batteries. No fewer than a dozen shipyards and designers were asked to submit designs for ironclads, for the one trump card the Admiralty could play to beat the French was the ability of the British shipbuilding industry to outbuild the French. In November 1858 the Naval Estimates presented to Parliament included a sum for the construction of two armored 'frigates.'

Once mobilized the mighty British shipbuilding industry

Below: The stern of the first British ironclad HMS *Warrior* as seen in a modern model.

swung into action with its usual efficiency. The first ironclad, the *Warrior* was laid down at Blackwall on the River Thames in May 1859 and launched the following December, not long after the completion of *La Gloire*'s trials. The *Black Prince* was slightly later, being launched on the Clyde in February 1861, and the two ships entered service in October 1861 and September 1862 respectively. They were not only seagoing ironclads but also the world's first iron-hulled ironclads, for the British had already built a class of iron-hulled floating batteries in 1855–56 and in addition had the best-equipped iron shipbuilding resources. In any race of this sort the French could not compete for they lacked the industrial capacity. Their first iron-hulled ship, *La Couronne*, although laid down more than a year ahead of the *Warrior* was launched a month after her.

There were important advantages in using iron. Most important was the possibility of providing watertight bulkheads, but it also produced a much stiffer hull which could carry the weight of heavier guns as well as the armor. The hull could be made longer for speed without undue risk of 'hogging' and 'sagging' as wooden hulls were likely to. Another weakness of a wooden hull was the need to keep the gunports close together (because the hull had to be kept short), which made it easier for a hit from a large-caliber shot to punch in the armor plates and so disable several guns in the battery.

The appearance of the slim and graceful *Warrior* and *Black*

Left: The rather unprepossessing profile of the *Gloire*.
Above right: The dented turret of the *Monitor* after the Battle of Hampton Roads.
Right: Section through *Monitor*'s turret.
Below: The *Monitor* as seen in a contemporary engraving.

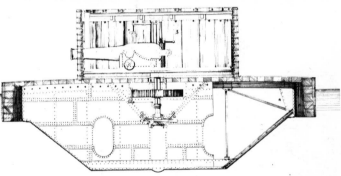

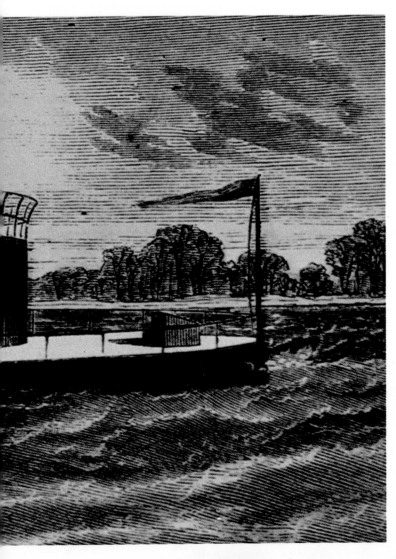

Prince in the Channel Squadron in 1862 did much to dispel the panic and helped to restore Anglo-French cordiality to some extent. The 'black snakes of the Channel' created a tremendous impression for unlike *La Gloire* they were remarkably handsome ships. Nor were they the only British ironclads. By 1866 another nine were completed, during which time the French Navy completed only two. Not only did French arsenals and shipyards lack the capacity for building rapidly but the demands for increased expenditure on the Army tended to siphon off the money which could have been spent on modern equipment for rolling armor plates and building steam machinery.

Neither *La Gloire* nor *Warrior* enjoyed their prestige for long. The following classes were even bigger and better protected, so big in fact that they became too unwieldy. Clearly the broadside ironclad could not develop much further and so designers turned to other means of providing the gunpower needed. One such idea was the cupola or turret, proposed in 1854 by John Ericsson, a Swedish engineer and also stumbled on in the Black Sea in 1855 by a Royal Navy captain, Cowper Coles. Coles had put a 32-pdr gun on a crude turntable on a raft, nicknamed the *Lady Nancy*, and in 1859 he produced plans for a gun-raft protected by an iron shield or cupola. The Navy liked his ideas and installed a prototype turret on the deck of the floating battery *Trusty* for firing trials in 1861. It was hit 33 times by heavy shells but continued to function. The Admiralty was convinced and drew up plans for turret-armed ironclads.

Events overtook the Admiralty's plans, for in 1861 the American Civil War broke out. The new Federal Navy's problems were acute, for by April 1861 it had not only lost the cream of its officers but also its main dockyard at Norfolk, Virginia. The Confederates found the new steam frigate *Merrimack*, lying

Above and top: The interior views of the monitor *Catskill*, an officer's cabin and the emergency steering position in the engine room.

engineer John Ericsson was on hand with his ideas for a turret-ship (last heard of in 1854). The Navy Department accepted his proposals promptly, and as speed was essential, Ericsson simplified the design as much as he could. His solution was the antithesis of the battery ship, an armored raft surmounted by a single revolving turret containing two 11-inch guns. Her name was to be *Monitor* 'that she might serve as a warning to others.'

The *Monitor* was commissioned on 25 February 1862, just four months after the contract had been signed. Even so she was nearly too late, for on the day she was due off Hampton Roads the *Merrimack* put to sea. The Confederate ironclad destroyed the wooden frigates *Cumberland* and *Congress* with apparent ease, showing just how helpless an unarmored sailing warship was against an ironclad.

Next morning the *Merrimack* reappeared, intent on finishing off the big screw frigate *Minnesota*, which had escaped destruction the previous day by running herself aground. At first she ignored the *Monitor* mistaking her for a water-tank when she was sighted alongside the *Minnesota*, but as soon as the 'cheese-box on a raft' opened fire with her 11-inch guns the Confederate ironclad switched targets and tried to dispose of this impudent intruder. Firing continued for about three and a half hours, the *Monitor* firing her guns every seven or eight minutes and the *Merrimack* taking 15 minutes for each broadside. The baffled Confederates eventually tried to ram but the little turret ship could turn in a sixth of the length needed by the clumsy *Merrimack*. When several attempts failed the *Merrimack* withdrew to her anchorage in the James River, and the Battle of Hampton Roads was over.

The two doughty opponents met again on 11 April but did not engage as Admiral Goldsborough had strict orders not to risk the *Monitor*. Just what might have happened if the *Monitor* had used a heavier charge than the scanty 15 pounds of powder allowed for her unproofed guns, or if the *Merrimack* had fired solid shot against her armor can only be guessed at, but the result of the action on 25 February confirmed the value of both armor plating and the revolving turret. Although often claimed to

burnt out and scuttled in the dockyard, but when the water-logged hulk was raised they were delighted to find that the machinery was still in good condition.

The problem faced by the Confederate Navy was the reverse of the position in the Crimean War; it was blockaded in its harbors by Union ships and under bombardment from land artillery. If the *Merrimack* could be turned into an armored battery she would be able to run the gauntlet of the Union artillery and smash her way through the unarmored blockading squadron and clear the approaches to the port.

By June 1861 work had started at Norfolk on rebuilding the ship, using railroad iron to build up a sloping casemate housing a battery of nine guns. Although renamed CSS *Virginia* she remained better known by her original name, and the work on her was completed by the early spring of 1862. The Federal authorities, aware of her existence, had in August 1861 authorized the construction of ironclads to match her but the problem remained of what to build. Fortunately the Swedish

have been the reason why other navies became enthusiastic, Hampton Roads merely provided public proof. Some days before the battle the Admiralty had in fact given approval to build two turret ships. Admiralty records mention their Lordships' pleasure at the news of Hampton Roads, for it meant that their decision was less likely to be publicly challenged.

In America there was understandable enthusiasm to build more and more *Monitors*, for the little ship gave her name to a new type. The Southern States could not match this with their primitive industries, but succeeded in building a second *Virginia* (to replace the *Merrimack* burned in May 1862) and the *Tennessee*. The *Virginia* was scuttled when Richmond was abandoned but the *Tennessee* fought Farragut's fleet at Mobile Bay in 1864, surrendering after being disabled by the monitor *Manhattan*. The monitors proved very useful on the big rivers but they were barely seaworthy; the *Monitor* very nearly foundered on the way down to Hampton Roads and did actually founder in a gale off Cape Hatteras at the end of 1862, while the *Weehawken* foundered in 1865. Although much bigger monitors were built, culminating in the 4400-ton *Dictator* armed with two 15-inch guns, they were no substitute for a seagoing fleet. Anti-British feeling in the North ran high as long as sympathy for the Southern cause persisted in Britain, but wild talk of sending the monitor fleet to settle scores with John Bull was ludicrous for they could never have fought their guns in the Atlantic.

Although most navies built monitors of various kinds the British were already moving to the next step, an ocean-going turret ship. In 1866 they ordered the *Monarch*, an 8000-ton fully rigged ship armed with four 11-inch guns in twin Coles turrets. Ever since the Battle of Hampton Roads the inventor had demanded that a turret battleship should be built, but when he saw the *Monarch* he was still not satisfied. Being a gunnery officer he could not accept her high freeboard, and wanted the lowest possible freeboard to give a 360 degree arc of fire. The Admiralty supported the Chief Surveyor, Edward Reed, in his claim that it was impossible to reconcile Coles' ideas with adequate seakeeping and stability but they reckoned without public opinion. By carefully orchestrating Parliamentary and Press support Coles was able to persuade the First Lord to let him design a second turret ship, to be called HMS *Captain*.

Not unnaturally Edward Reed, widely regarded as one of the two greatest living naval architects, took it as a slur on his department's competence, especially as Coles had no technical qualifications. The Navy's attitude was that Coles would have a free hand to advise and consult with the builders, the Laird brothers, but the customary supervision of construction by Admiralty overseers would not be allowed. In such an atmosphere the *Captain* took shape, and when she was launched in March 1869 it was discovered that she was considerably overweight. Coles was not particularly perturbed and showed no inclination to reduce the great spread of canvas the ship was to carry. Finally she went to sea in January 1870, and to show official approval the First Lord of the Admiralty Sir Hugh Childers announced that his only son would sail in her as a midshipman.

All went well for the first three months and the ship's officers expressed great satisfaction with her. But suddenly on the night of 6 September 1870, while the Channel Squadron was beset by a gale, HMS *Captain* was swept over on her beam ends and then capsized. So rapid was the disaster than only seven out of the 473 men aboard escaped. Among those who went down with her were Captain Coles and the midshipman son of Hugh Childers.

In the uproar that followed a searching enquiry revealed that HMS *Captain* had foundered from the 'pressure of sail assisted by the heave of the sea.' Edward Reed, however, was amply vindicated when his *Monarch* proved an outstanding success, but what was really at stake was the need to take professional ship-designers seriously. The process was already moving slowly and the loss of the *Captain* did no more than hasten it, but 1870 marked the end of the first experimental phase in the evolution of the battleship.

Below: The *Roanoke*, the only US monitor built with three turrets. The monitors were not suitable for long ocean voyages.

SOVEREIGNS OF THE SEAS

The *Captain* disaster did nothing to slow up developments, and throughout the 1870s navies built a bewildering variety of types in an effort to find the best solution. The spur was the need to protect ships against the newest guns, for with metallurgy making rapid advances it was just as easy to improve guns as it was to improve armor. As early as 1853 the British had introduced a rifled gun, in which the shell was forced into the rifling by the explosion of the charge. Their worst drawback was the amount of 'windage' or the gap between the shell and barrel needed to allow the shell to be loaded, but they were cheap and simple to operate.

Breech-loading offered the chance to overcome windage and in 1859 William Armstrong demonstrated his system to the Admiralty. He used a removable breech-block to close the chamber behind the charge and then rammed it tight by means of a hollow screw, through which the shell and charge had already been passed. There was strong support from Press and Parliament once again and the Armstrong gun was adopted promptly the same year. But once again things went wrong, not as disastrously as with HMS *Captain*, but demonstrating just as clearly what happens when public pressure takes over from professional judgment.

The disaster was the bombardment of Kagoshima on 15 August 1863 when a British squadron tried to exact an indemnity from the Daimyo of Satsuma for the murder of an English merchant. The action was distinguished by a series of gun-accidents which showed that the Armstrong was unreliable. In an action lasting two hours 21 Armstrong guns fired 365 rounds and suffered an aggregate of 28 accidents, the worst being when a 7-inch gun in the flagship blew out its breech-block and concussed the entire gun crew.

The answer was to change to the French system of 'shunt rifling' and muzzle-loading, for the Royal Navy could not afford any more expensive experiments which might involve reequipping the entire fleet. The French themselves had decided to change to breech-loading but they had adopted a hinged threaded block, without the separate breech block which had caused all the problems in the Armstrong gun. The threaded block took so many turns to open and shut that the logical improvement was to cut away every sixth part of the threads; it needed only a sixth-turn to shut it and yet it retained the strength of the fully threaded block. Friedrich Krupp preferred to use a sliding block breech-loading system but all three systems, British, French and German now strengthened their gun barrels by shrinking hoops on them, as first proposed by Armstrong.

Guns now got much bigger. At the end of the Crimean War the biggest gun afloat was a 10-inch 84-pdr. Armstrong produced a 13-inch 600-pdr and at the end of the Civil War the monitor *Puritan* was going to receive two 20-inch Dahlgren guns. The breech-loaders also grew rapidly in size and weight; the 7-inch 110-pdr Armstrong weighed a mere 4 tons whereas the 13-inch 600-pdr weighed 22 tons, causing many more problems in handling. A whole variety of devices came into use to control the recoil of such monsters and steam and hydraulic training were developed for the mountings.

The French did not favor the turret, preferring to develop the *barbette*, a circular iron shield inside which the guns

Right: The forward 12-inch turret of the USS *Mississippi* pictured in 1908. The *Mississippi* carried two such turrets.
Below: A painting of the battleship USS *Iowa*, showing her as she would have appeared in 1898.

revolved. Its advantage was that it weighed less than the turret since the training machinery was only turning the guns rather than the whole mass of the armored turret. In turn this meant that guns could be carried higher above the waterline than in turret ships, and from the end of the 1860s a number of French ships were fitted with four single guns in barbettes disposed 'lozenge' fashion (one forward, one aft and two port and starboard amidships). The British found a different solution, in the 'central battery,' shortening the side armor in order to give heavier protection to a central 'casemate' amidships. This arrangement not only saved length but with recessed gunports allowed the guns to fire closer to the centerline. One of the weaknesses of the older broadside ironclads was this lack of end-on fire, and many expedients were adopted to provide bow- and stern-chase guns.

The biggest problem was lack of experience on which practical design ideas could be based. The Civil War was recognized to have been a special case never likely to recur, while the Crimean War had even less relevance. But on 20 July 1866 the Austrians and Italians fought off the Island of Lissa in the Adriatic, and this action was to have as much influence as Hampton Roads. Not only was it the first full fleet action fought in European waters since Trafalgar but also the first battle involving seagoing ironclads. The newly unified Italian state had joined Prussia in furthering Bismarck's plans to acquire part of the Austro-Hungarian Empire. The Austro-Hungarian Fleet under Rear-Admiral Wilhelm von Tegetthoff had only seven armored ships out of a total of 27, against Count Carlo Pellion de Persano's 12 out of a total of 34, but there was a vast difference in the standard of leadership and training. The Italians had spared no expense to create a new fleet, including a new turret ram, the *Affondatore*, and could bring 200 modern rifled guns into action aginst the 74 in Tegetthoff's fleet.

Below: HMS *Agincourt* was built with the unusual number of five masts but is seen here after two had been removed.

Faced with such opposition Tegetthoff could either avoid action or trust in superior seamanship and tactics. He chose the latter, knowing full well that Persano was an indecisive leader with poorly trained men. He ordered his ships to close the range so that the older muzzle-loaders could penetrate the Italians' armor and instructed them to ram enemy ships whenever possible, to throw the Italian battle-line into confusion: 'ironclads will dash at the enemy and sink him.' Tegetthoff's three divisions attacked in an arrowhead formation and achieved his primary objective by slipping through a gap in the Italian line. Although ramming proved almost impossible because of the clumsiness of the ships and the dense clouds of powder-smoke the attempts produced a fierce melée.

The decisive moment came when Tegetthoff in his flagship *Ferdinand Max* sighted the *Re d'Italia* through a gap in the smoke. The big Italian frigate had been disabled by a shell-hit in the rudder and could do nothing to escape her fate as the *Ferdinand Max* bore down on her. The iron spur under the forefoot struck the *Re d'Italia* full amidship and tore an enormous hole on the waterline. The *Ferdinand Max* then reversed her screws and pulled away, ripping an even larger hole. The doomed Italian ship sagged slowly over to starboard as hundreds of tons of water rushed into her hull, righted momentarily and then rolled the other way and capsized, taking 662 men with her. The only other casualty of the battle was the ironclad *Palestro*, which blew up after being set on fire by the *Ferdinand Max* early on, but the Italians had had enough. After a show of bravado by hoisting a signal for 'General Chase' Persano withdrew to Ancona and left the field to Tegetthoff.

The real lesson of Lissa was that poor maneuverability and inaccurate guns made it very difficult to sink ships in battle, but the world's navies seized on the ramming of the *Re d'Italia* as proof that the ram would be decisive. For another 30 years battleships would be built with massive reinforced stems for ramming tactics, achieving little apart from spectacular collisions with their squadron-mates. And yet we can now see

Above: HMS *Inflexible* tried to combine ahead and astern fire with a small area of armor by mounting the two turrets *en echelon* amidships. This arrangement was not successful.
Left: HMS *Devastation*, the most successful 1870s design.

the field, followed by the French, but before long both Germany and Russia developed the capacity to build ironclads. For the time being the other industrial giant, the United States, was content to ignore these developments, as the aftermath of the Civil War focussed energies on developing internal resources rather than maritime power. There was also the understandable tendency to assume that the large fleet of monitors was sufficient investment in sea power for the time being. The magnitude of that error would become apparent later, but without the threat of a naval war to disturb the complacency of the politicians in Washington there was little that anyone could have done to change matters.

It was left to the British to show the way ahead. In 1869, while the *Captain* was still fitting out and the *Monarch* had just gone to sea, Parliament voted for three more large turret ships. With the reputation of the US Navy's monitors standing very high, Sir Edward Reed chose a low freeboard ship with two large twin turrets protected by an armored 'breastwork' and no sails of any sort. The arrival of the USS *Miantonomoh* at Portsmouth in 1867 lent some credence to American claims of the big monitors' seaworthiness but eyewitness accounts testify to the hellish conditions aboard when she first arrived. Then came the disaster of the *Captain*, a year after the keels of the first two of the new turret ships were laid, and a storm of protest arose. To settle doubts about their design the First Lord of the Admiralty appointed a Committee on Designs. When it met in January 1871 Reed had already resigned as Chief Constructor, to take up a job in industry and so it had little difficulty in recommending certain changes to the design of the new ships. But what was much more important was the recommendation that sail power should be abolished for large warships. It was recognized that a 'very high degree of offensive and defensive power' could not be combined with real efficiency under sail. Although later ships were to carry masts and yards they did so to save coal on long cruises by 'easing' the engines; the age of fighting under sail was over.

HMS *Devastation* went to sea in the spring of 1873 under a cloud of suspicion and pessimism never seen before or since. An anonymous hand even placed a notice by the gangway on the day of her commissioning: 'Letters for the *Captain* may be posted here.' But she confounded the critics when she was

that Lissa actually proved the opposite. Over and over again ramming attempts by Tegetthoff's ships had been defeated, and the solitary success had only been achieved because the victim was unable to steer.

There was very little to help the designer in formulating requirements, and a confused and contradictory battle like Lissa was very little guidance. The two lessons learned, the need for end-on fire and a strengthened ram bow, were the wrong ones, but indirectly they proved a positive influence. More emphasis was placed on handiness and inevitably the revolving turret was vindicated as it offered the widest arcs of fire. But there were to be many quaint compromise solutions to the problem during the 1870s; turret rams, casemate ships, box-battery ships and more of the monitor type. All of them looked like the freaks that they were, often with huge exaggerated rams. There were ships with two turrets side by side on the forecastle, turrets *en echelon* amidships and combinations of central batteries and barbettes, in a bewildering profusion of types. There was no war nor even a serious threat of a war (in Europe at any rate) and this 'fleet of samples' was more a reflection of the industrial growth of Europe than any expression of tactical doctrine.

Battleship design, with its need for even harder armor plate, bigger forgings for guns and the most powerful machinery, made heavy demands on technology. At first the British had dominated sent out into the Eastern Atlantic with the old broadside iron-clad *Agincourt* and the new central battery ship *Sultan*. She behaved as well or better in a variety of sea states and she was in no danger of capsizing. Naturally her low freeboard imposed some limitations, for it was impossible to prevent water from finding its way down below the forecastle, but there was no doubt that she could steam and fight in the Atlantic. She and her sister *Thunderer* also carried nearly 2000 tons of coal and could steam some 5000 miles at cruising speed. The lack of sail power gave the guns maximum arcs of fire ahead and on the beam and reduced the size of the crew considerably. Without the weight of heavy masts and standing rigging the hull was also steadier and a greater proportion of weight could be devoted to armor, coal and habitability.

In 1872 the Italian Navy laid down two large battleships, the *Duilio* and *Dandolo*, intended to have the thickest armor and the largest guns. The designer, Benedetto Brin had considerable talent and his first proposal for ships with four 38-ton 12.5-inch guns would have given the Italians two ships well able to deal with any opposition in the Mediterranean.

Problems only started when Armstrongs offered the Italian Navy its latest 60-ton 15-inch gun. No sooner was the offer accepted than Armstrongs raised the bidding with a 100-ton 17.7-inch, and Brin was told to alter his design accordingly. He was forced to recast the design entirely, choosing a 'raft body' underwater, on which the ship would be able to float if the remaining two-thirds of the ship were flooded. The basic concept was sound enough but the immense size of the guns made nonsense of it. The light hull could not take the stresses of continuous firing, and as the 100-tonners fired so slowly and inaccurately the ship could easily be riddled by shells from lighter and faster-firing guns before she could reply. The Italian answer to these criticisms was beguilingly simple: they knew that the *Duilio* and *Dandolo* would not show up too well in a ship-to-ship combat but if given sufficient speed they might be able to stay out of trouble.

In 1874 the official 'reply' to the Italian ships, HMS *Inflexible* was laid down. She resembled the *Duilio* in having two turrets *en echelon* amidships, a raft body and central 'citadel' protected by 24 inches of compound steel and iron armor. The Admiralty did not try to match the Armstrong 100-ton gun, preferring the Woolwich 80-ton 16-inch. This gun marked the peak of rifled muzzle-loader development. The

Above: The German turret ship *Friedrich der Grosse* (1877) carried four 10.2-inch guns and could steam at 14 knots.
Above right: HMS *Thunderer* in 1891 after being rearmed with breechloading 10-inch guns.
Below right: The *Andrea Doria* and her sisters were slight improvements on the *Duilo* and *Dandolo*.
Below: The armored corvette *Baden* and her sisters were built in 1875–83. They carried six 10.2-inch guns.

had thought out any task for her to perform, her sole claim to fame was to be commanded by Captain John Fisher at the bombardment of Alexandria in 1882. She fired 88 rounds and was hit by a single 10-inch shell which inflicted considerably less damage than the blast of her own 16-inch guns.

Undaunted by the shortcomings of the *Duilio* and *Dandolo*, Benedetto Brin went on to build much improved versions, the *Italia* and *Lepanto*. This time the guns were 103-ton 17-inch breech-loaders, and instead of two turrets he sited them in a heavily armored 'redoubt' resembling the French barbette system. They were technical masterpieces but were overtaken by two events, the introduction of high explosive shells and quick-firing guns. Now it was possible to inflict great damage on unarmored structures with comparatively light guns (mostly 4-inch to 6-inch). Ships like *Italia* and *Inflexible* would be put out of action even if they could not be sunk.

There was a revolution brewing in the world of big guns as well. In 1878 Sir Andrew Noble and Professor Abel began a series of experiments which proved that ballistics would be improved with slower-burning gunpowder. This in turn called for longer barrels to ensure that the powder burned for as long as possible. Other improvements were to make the gunpowder in large or 'pebble' grains and to chamber the breech to improve combustion. All this led to agitation for a return to breech-loading, for longer guns were very difficult to load from the muzzle-end. In 1875 Krupp had introduced his 'mantle-ring' system, shrinking a jacket over the breech-end to provide much

barrels were too long to be run back into the turret for loading and instead the muzzles were depressed below an armored 'glacis' on the deck to allow first the charge and then the shell to be rammed upwards.

Inflexible was a triumph of mechanical ingenuity, the first battleship lit by electricity, the first with anti-rolling tanks, the thickest armor ever, and above all, the first design to be thoroughly tested and discussed before building started. And yet she was a failure; because there was no Naval Staff nobody

greater strength than before, and no muzzle-loader could match the extra power. Excessive parsimony had prevented the Royal Navy from considering such innovations for the best part of a decade, but a growing awareness that the European navies could overtake the British loosened the purse strings at last.

In April 1879 a committee was set up to consider a revival of the breech-loader and at the same time a group of technicians went to Meppen to witness trials of the new Krupp guns. They returned full of enthusiasm and the Admiralty wasted no further time in ordering a new breech-loading 12-inch. The French interrupted screw method was adopted rather than the Krupp sliding breech, with several safety interlocks in an effort to prevent accidents.

Once the decision was made to revert to breech-loaders the Royal Navy planned a new series of ships to match the latest French barbette ships. The first was HMS *Collingwood* which used the layout of the *Devastation* with the four 12-inch breech-loaders in twin barbettes on the French style. The protection was limited to a short but thick belt on the waterline, closed at either end by a transverse bulkhead. The ends were left 'soft' or unarmored, on the assumption that as long as the central 'citadel' remained intact the ship would float with both ends flooded. Although her 12-inch guns looked somewhat less imposing than the older muzzle-loaders they were much more efficient and enhanced her neat, functional appearance. Five more improved *Collingwoods* were built, four with four new 30-ton 13.5-inch guns and one, HMS *Benbow*, with two 111-ton 16.25-inch guns. The decision to go for another 'monster gun' was a mistake, for with one round fired every 3–4 minutes the *Benbow* was less likely to score a hit than a ship armed with twice as many lighter guns.

Below: Sir William White's *Royal Sovereign* established the layout used for all British battleships up to the revolutionary *Dreadnought* design.

The 1880s and 1890s saw a remarkable upsurge of public interest in naval affairs, in Great Britain, Europe and the United States, with naval yearbooks and journals providing more information about warship designs, armaments and fleet strengths. The debates about design had hitherto been confined to the administration and technicians, except when a disaster brought the problems into the public arena, but from now until World War I respective naval strengths would be a matter of public concern. Newspapers and books bombarded their readers with information about trials of new guns and armor plates, and as all the underlying tensions came closer to the surface a note of strident nationalism pervaded it all. The closing years of the nineteenth century became the Age of the Battleship, with rival strengths reckoned in numbers of battleships, but little thought given to broader strategic and technical matters.

There was, for example, the question of the Whitehead torpedo, a self-propelled explosive device which could blow a hole in a ship's side. The Royal Navy had enthusiastically snapped up the invention in the early 1870s without thinking too hard about how best to use it. But, by the mid-1880s, small fast torpedo boats had been built in sufficient numbers to threaten any battleships trying to lie off an enemy harbor. This made any repetition of the classic blockade of the French Fleet by Cornwallis a thing of the past, and some supporters of the torpedo boat even dared to predict that the battleship had no future.

Despite these criticisms the 'Admiral' Class was chosen as the basis for a new class of big ships to be built under a massive program authorized by the 1889 Naval Defence Act. Growing public agitation about the alleged weaknesses of the Royal Navy had forced the Conservative Government's hand. Had the critics known, the British position was not as bad as they had assumed, for the French Chamber of Deputies had been told in 1886 that only ten battleships were ready to go to sea. Out of six ships started between 1878 and 1881 only one was nearing completion and another was less than 40 per cent complete after five years'

Above: SMS *Kurfurst Friedrich Wilhelm* (1893) saw service in the early months of WWI but was then laid up and her crew transferred to more modern ships.
Right: The USS *Illinois* (BB.7) seen being prepared for docking in January 1902.

work. The French still had most of their timber-hulled ironclads from the 1860s on the strength whereas such ships as HMS *Warrior* had virtually been pensioned off.

The new design, the *Royal Sovereign* Class, matched the scale of the program, with the freeboard which the 'Admirals' lacked. Seven were barbette ships, carrying their four 13.5-inch guns in open-topped mountings, but as a stop to the objections of the elderly First Sea Lord, Sir Arthur Hood, an eighth unit was built with turrets instead of barbettes. The case was finally proven; the *Hood* had less freeboard and so could never make the speed of her half-sisters in bad weather.

The impetus given by the Naval Defence Act was not lost, and the next class of nine ships, the *Majestics*, were even more impressive. The layout of the *Royal Sovereigns* was retained but

Below: The USS *Kearsarge* had her secondary guns mounted directly over her main armament – an unusual and unsuccessful arrangement. She is seen here in 1899.

the barbettes were given armored hoods – the term 'hooded barbette' eventually became 'turret' when the old pillbox-type had disappeared – and all the 6-inch guns were protected by armored casemates. The *Majestics* were even better-looking than the previous ships, so much so that the US Navy paid them the compliment of copying the look for their *Alabama* Class. It was not only the fighting qualities of the *Majestic* Class that amazed other navies; the lead-ship was built by Portsmouth Dockyard in under 22 months, a world record. In less than ten years the Royal Navy was strengthened by 16 first-class battleships, whereas France and Germany completed only 6, and Russia and the United States 4 each.

The French Navy went into comparative decline at the end of the century, partly because of the patent hopelessness of trying to outbuild the British, partly because of mischievous political meddling, but largely because of the influence of the 'Young School' or *Jeune Ecole*. There were influential naval officers who believed that torpedo boats had made the battleship obsolete and that destruction of commerce was a more certain way to beat the British than fighting their Fleet. But in place of the French appeared a much more dangerous rival, the German Navy. Starting from a coast defense force, its strength was built up by a series of Navy Acts intended to provide a firm basis for replacing obsolescent tonnage. Dreams of naval expansion pandered to nationalist sentiments in a way that mere totals of money could not. They also alarmed the British, who saw clearly that the enlarged German Navy could only threaten their own position. With jingoism and tension rampant in all the leading nations of Europe it was not the moment to start a naval arms race but Admiral Tirpitz could not see this. Protesting all the while that the new battleships were essential to protect German interests, he ordered 20 large battleships between 1890 and 1905. The argument was quite simply that battleships were a measure of national prestige, and as Germany was a strong industrial nation she needed a fleet of appropriate size. A second reason

Below: HMS *Caesar* of the *Majestic* Class, regarded as the best of
Sir William White's designs. She is seen in the standard Victorian
color scheme of black hull, white upperworks and buff funnels.
Far right, top: The monitor USS *Amphitrite* (1895) and her sisters
were totally unsuited for any but the shortest-range operations.

was Germany's desperate need for powerful allies; Tirpitz reasoned that a big enough fleet would make Germany a desirable ally.

The US Navy had expanded very little since 1866 for Congress refused consistently to sanction any major warships, on the grounds that battleships and big cruisers would lead to 'international adventures.' Far-sighted officers and administrators tried as early as 1874 to get some measure of new building put in hand but they were only able to get grudging permission to repair old monitors. To circumvent this they used money voted to repair five Civil War monitors to build five new ships. As material had to be ordered surreptitiously the work took from 17 to 22 years to complete.

The first battleships allowed to be built were the small 2nd class units *Texas* and *Maine* (the latter was first conceived as an armored cruiser) ordered in 1886. Four years later three battleships, *Indiana*, *Massachusetts* and *Oregon* were ordered, but with only 12 feet of freeboard and 400 tons of coal they were hardly fit for more than coastal defense. The next ship, the *Iowa* was hardly any better, and until the three *Alabama* Class were laid down in 1896–7 the US Navy could not boast a single battleship capable of facing the latest European models.

Russia was in a worse state than France, with a slow building rate and a tendency to pack too many features into a small hull. Recognition of some of the basic weaknesses led the Russians to seek French advice on design, and from them they acquired many theories of design. The Russian sailor and his officers were brave but lacked good professional training, while the innate corruption of the system made the task of reform hopeless.

To an outside observer the front-line navies at the end of the century appeared marvels of precision and smartness. There was as yet no suggestion that color-schemes should be chosen for anything but appearance, and the long lines of black hulls,

white upperworks and buff funnels impressed civilians. After 30 years of peace, 'spit and polish' had been given too much priority over such matters as gunnery and tactics, but we should not underestimate the seamanship and skills of late nineteenth century battleship captains. Gunnery was practised at no more than 4000 yards, little more than the extreme range of Nelson's 32-pounders at Trafalgar, but this was because irregular-burning powders produced a wide scatter of shots at extreme ranges. At a range of 7000 yards or more the only thing visible with the naked eye was a plume of smoke from the target's funnels and the 100-feet high splash of a 12-inch shell.

Much nonsense has been written about officers throwing shells overboard to avoid the tedium of gunnery drills, and the facts are that by the end of the century the front-line navies were all in a state of reasonable efficiency. But it was all to be made to look obsolescent by a veritable hurricane of change which was to transform them beyond recognition.

GUNNERY AND THE DREADNOU

The problem of all nineteenth century battleship-designers was that they were denied all but a few tantalizing fragments of experience. All their theories of gun layout and armor distribution rested on the experience of the Crimean War, Lissa and half a dozen minor actions. Not until 1904 did modern warships meet their equals, when the Japanese clashed with the Russians over which one was to dominate Manchuria. At the end of the war the Russian Pacific Fleet had been sunk at its moorings by long-range gunfire and the Baltic Fleet had been annihilated at the Battle of Tsushima in May 1905, the first full fleet action since Lissa.

The Japanese had deliberately courted war for they were determined to stop Russia from establishing a foothold in Manchuria. The powerful fortified base at Port Arthur was a constant thorn in their flesh and when it was announced that the Port Arthur fleet would be increased from seven to thirteen battleships by the end of 1905 the Japanese decided to strike first. They had only six modern battleships and it seemed foolish to wait until the Russian superiority was doubled.

On the night of 8 February 1904 ten destroyers attacked Port Arthur and damaged two battleships and a cruiser with torpedoes. This foretaste of Pearl Harbor gave the Japanese Fleet only a temporary advantage and a great fillip to their confidence. The Russians never gained the iniative thereafter, and when the energetic Admiral Makarov was drowned in his flagship *Petropavlovsk* after she had struck a mine, the fighting spirit of the Port Arthur squadron seemed to wither away. Not even the sinking of two Japanese battleships in a minefield tempted the Russians; an attempt to break out in August 1904 was the last sign of any activity and four months later 11-inch howitzers belonging to General Nogi's besieging army sank the surviving ships at their moorings.

Meanwhile the Russian Baltic Fleet had begun its incredible odyssey, steaming around the world to try to save Port Arthur. Vice-Admiral Rozhdestvenski's fleet ploughed on around the Cape of Good Hope and despite the dispiriting news of the surrender of Port Arthur continued its seven-month journey

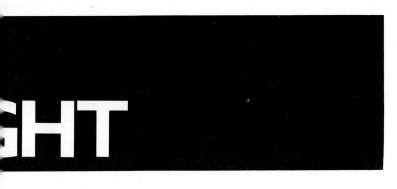

GHT

and approached the Japanese islands with the intention of either brushing past Admiral Togo's fleet to reach Vladivostok or bringing it to action and destroying it. With eight battleships, three coast defense ships, three big armored cruisers, six light cruisers and ten destroyers Rozhdestvenski seemed to have a powerful advantage over Togo's four battleships, seven armored cruisers and seven light cruisers. But Togo's ships could steam together at 15 knots whereas the Russians had a combined speed of only 12 knots and there was no comparison between the standards of training in the two fleets.

Early on the morning of 27 May 1905 Togo's scouts sighted the Baltic Fleet entering the Straits of Tsushima but it was noon before Togo decided to bring his big ships into action. The Russians were already in line ahead, the four modern ships leading, and Togo turned to port to bring his own line around on a course nearly parallel. The Russians replied with fierce but inaccurate fire at a range of about 6500 yards, and failed to prevent Togo from concentrating his fire against the head of the line. By 1400 the flagship *Kniaz Suvorov* was under heavy fire from several ships and Vice-Admiral Rozhdestvenski had been badly wounded by a shell-splinter. The Russian second division, comprising four older battleships, was under heavy fire from the Japanese armored cruisers and eventually the *Oslyabya* was reduced to a sinking condition by numerous hits.

The flagship drifted off from her consorts, shrouded in smoke from internal fires. A hit from a destroyer's torpedo failed to stop her and three hours later she was still fighting off attacks. At about 1730 a destroyer took off the badly wounded Admiral but still the smoke-blackened wreck fired her light guns and

The Russian battleship *Oslyabya* was sunk at Tsushima. This photograph gives a good impression of the high sides and tumble-home which were a feature of many late nineteenth century designs.

Above: Rozhdestvensky's advance to Tsushima.
Below: The 12,900 ton *Tsarevitch*, sister ship of the *Borodino*.

kept the Japanese destroyers and torpedo boats at bay. Finally at 1920 a division of torpedo boats scored two or three hits and ended the agony; the *Kniaz Suvorov* rolled over on her side and went down with all 928 officers and men.

Meanwhile the *Borodino* led the survivors of the battleline in a forlorn attempt to break out of the trap. At about the same time as the sinking of the flagship she was set on fire and her magazines blew up. The *Alexander III* had already capsized after repeated hits from 12-inch shells, leaving only the *Orel* and a handful of older ships circling aimlessly. The Japanese steamed around them firing at will, hampered only by the dense clouds of smoke. When the sun rose next morning the *Orel* and the other survivors could do nothing more and so they surrendered. The only ships to escape were a few which had chosen internment in neutral ports. It was the first complete victory since Trafalgar, the tactician's dream of a 'battle of annihilation. Japan suddenly became a world power and the Russians were reduced (albeit temporarily) to second-class status.

There were many lessons to be learned from Tsushima, but as always many wrong conclusions were drawn. The outstanding feature to most commentators was the 'immense' range at which fire had been opened, 7000 yards instead of half that distance, as had been customary. However, all but a few observers failed to notice that Japanese gunnery had been rapid rather than accurate and only when the range came down considerably and the target had been disabled did the number of hits start to increase.

Another popular misconception was the psychological effect of high-explosive or 'common' shells exploding. Many naval observers claimed that the concussion alone would demoralize an enemy and even advocated using them in place of armor-piercing shells. Not for another 11 years would it be rediscovered that superficial damage does not sink ships, and only penetration below the waterline or a hit in a magazine can sink a ship quickly. Another point overlooked was that the aggressive tactics used so successfully by the Japanese depended largely on the slow speed of the Russians and their inability to maneuver in unison.

The surrendered Russian ships and those raised in Port Arthur after the capture of the fortress yielded much valuable information, and even the Japanese ships damaged in action showed several shortcomings in design. British technical experts were allowed to inspect some of the ships in Japanese dockyards and the reports drew attention to the need for better pumping arrangements to prevent progressive flooding. Another fault which came to light was the poor quality of the Japanese armor-piercing shell; its Shimose burster was so sensitive that it detonated the shell when it struck the armor, rather than after penetration. The defect had been spotted earlier and was supposed to have been rectified but many of the Tsushima prizes showed that Japanese shells had burst outside the armor.

The excellent work done by the Japanese armored cruisers obscured the fact that they had been dealing with slow and weakly protected old battleships. A modern armored cruiser was in many ways superior to some older battleships and Admiral Kamimura's big cruisers had done sterling work against Rozhdestvenski's second and third divisions, composed of ships inferior in almost every aspect. It is doubtful if they would have had such a free hand if the Russian battleline had been properly screened by a mixed force of destroyers and cruisers.

The main reason for paying too little attention to the lessons of Tsushima was the conviction held by the major navies that they were already moving into a new era of technology. Certainly the ships engaged at Tsushima were obsolescent in comparison with the latest battleships on the drawing board in Britain, Germany and the United States and so it was understandable that less attention was paid to their behavior in battle. Many of the new concepts were apparently vindicated by Tsushima and the minor details were dismissed as irrelevant; unfortunately it was these 'minor' details which in the long run caused more trouble than anything else.

The new ideas were basically connected with the need to hit at longer range. Improvements in powder had already made it possible to increase the length of guns and so improve their ballistics, but at the end of the century there was another technological change, which went almost unnoticed.

The torpedo had been in service since 1870 but while it had a range of only 800 yards at 30 knots it held very few terrors for battleships on the high seas. The introduction of the heater system, however, pushed up range enormously to 3000 yards and more. This corresponded roughly to contemporary battle-ranges, making it necessary for the first time to open fire at much longer ranges. This effect on battle tactics is very rarely mentioned in connection with the sudden increase in battle ranges which took place in all leading navies at the turn of the century and yet it was by far the most important factor. The only drawback was that contemporary gunnery training methods and fire control lagged far behind and the first attempts to fire at longer ranges were disappointing.

Vital reforms in training were needed to push up the Royal Navy's average performance dramatically. There were no radar sets and only comparatively crude optical rangefinders so there was only one way to range on a distant target; spotting the shell-splashes of each salvo. With a battleship firing her four 12-inch guns every 2–3 minutes it was clearly difficult to range on a target if either or both ships were moving at high speed. It was also very hard to distinguish the splash made by a 6-inch shell from a 12-inch at great distances since both shells made very large splashes.

The first solution was to strengthen the main armament by

Right: Plan of the early phase of the Battle of Tsushima.
Below: The Japanese *Hatsuse* seen in 1901. She was sunk by a Russian mine in May 1904.

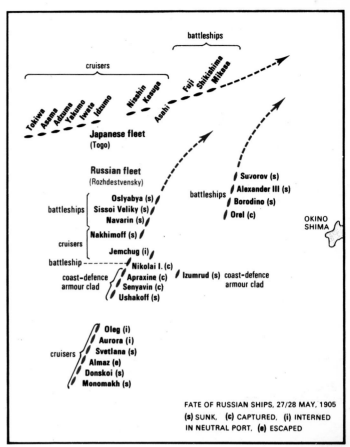

FATE OF RUSSIAN SHIPS, 27/28 MAY, 1905
(s) SUNK, **(c)** CAPTURED, **(i)** INTERNED
IN NEUTRAL PORT, **(e)** ESCAPED

installing an 'intermediate' battery of guns – these ranged from 6.7-inch in German ships to 7-inch and 8-inch in US ships, and finally in 1901 the British followed the trend by putting 9.2-inch in the *King Edward VII* Class. This caused more headaches because the shell-splash was even harder to distinguish from a 12-inch and because the blast from such large guns tended to make it hard to man searchlights and light guns nearby. The British went one better in the *Lord Nelson* and *Agamemnon*, omitting all the 6-inch guns and increasing the secondary armament to ten 9.2-inch but the Americans went even further ordering two ships with eight 12-inch guns and no intermediate guns of any sort.

This was the best solution of all. With four twin turrets a battleship could fire salvos from alternate guns, keeping up a good rate of fire to compensate for the 'rate of change' in relative positions. Four shells in a salvo offered a reasonable chance of hitting, provided the salvo was 'bracketed' around the target. The two ships, the USS *Michigan* and *South Carolina*, were given a most logical arrangement of guns, four twin turrets on the centerline, two forward and two aft with No 2 and No 3 superimposed to fire over No 1 and No 4 respectively. Quite by chance the 1903 edition of *Jane's Fighting Ships* published an article by the Italian designer General Cuniberti, proposing an 'ideal ship for the British Navy' armed with twelve 12-inch guns, protected by 12-inch armor and steaming at 23 knots.

The decision to order the two American ships in 1903, coming on top of the increase in torpedo-range and the recommendations of gunnery experts had considerably more influence on the British Admiralty than a sketch design in *Jane's*. Determined not to be left behind, in total secrecy the British designed a revolutionary new battleship to be called *Dreadnought* and hoped to be able to use their superior shipbuilding capacity to regain the lead. The leading influence in this plan was the new First Sea Lord, Sir John Fisher, who wished to enlarge the Royal Navy to meet the challenge from the rapidly growing German Navy. He followed the American lead in restricting the secondary armament to a battery of light guns to fight off torpedo craft but he went much further in adopting the new steam turbine in place of the old reciprocating engines.

The argument in favor of the turbine really rested on power

Above: Admiral Togo, victor at Tsushima.
Below: Togo's flagship *Mikasa* was the newest Japanese battleship and resembled contemporary British designs with twin funnels and casemated secondary armament.

Above: The *Shikishima* and her sister *Hatsuse* were built in Britain. She survived as a training hulk until 1947.

output. True, reciprocating engines had once been run in conditions which made the engine room a 'cross between an inferno and a snipe marsh' but they were now economical and clean thanks to forced lubrication and balanced crankshafts. The real problem was that any major increase of power to give higher speed (say 3 knots) would need nearly 50 per cent more power, and such an increase would increase the volume of the machinery enormously. Fortunately the British were in the lead of turbine development, having put the Parsons turbine in four destroyers and a light cruiser. The Cunard line was about to instal Parsons turbines in a big transatlantic liner and the Engineer-in-Chief was confident that the *Dreadnought* could reach 21 knots; three knots more than the *Lord Nelson*.

To pull together all the diverse strands Fisher appointed a very highly qualified Committee on Designs, whose terms of reference were to consider the design of a battleship armed with 12-inch guns and anti-torpedo boat armament, no intermediate guns, and 21 knots' speed and 'adequate' armor. From the first meeting on 3 January 1905 it was clear that Fisher had already decided what sort he wanted, and there was very little real discussion about alternatives. Yet Fisher seems to have had little idea of the implications of long-range gunnery as he still maintained that hits at 6000 yards and more would only be obtained by firing single shots slowly. Several arrangements of guns were considered in an attempt to get six twin 12-inch but in each case size and cost proved prohibitive. Finally design 'H' was accepted, and reciprocating engines were replaced by turbines at the last minute. When the Committee handed in its report on 22 February it had finalized the most revolutionary warship design since the *Warrior* in just seven weeks.

There were surprisingly few mistakes for such a hurriedly designed ship. Siting the boats between the two funnels meant that the masthead control platform stood directly over the forefunnel and was usually blanketed by smoke when the ship steamed at full speed. Political pressure to keep size down eliminated a strake of 8-inch side armor above the main 11-inch belt which had been provided in the *Lord Nelson*, making the new ship vulnerable to shellfire when the side belt was immersed at maximum draught. Against these criticisms she had several minor innovations and there was much internal weight saving. As it was intended to build the ship as quickly as possible structures were kept simple. The variety of steel sections was kept to the minimum and wherever possible standard-sized plates were used. Finally a large amount of material was prepared in advance and the four 12-inch turrets already building for the *Lord Nelson* and *Agamemnon* were requisitioned.

With such elaborate attempts to cut down building time it was to be expected that the new battleship would be built in record time, but even so the rate of construction was staggering and it constitutes a record which has never been broken. The keel was laid on Monday 2 October 1905 and only a week later the main deck beams were in place. By the end of December the hull was almost complete and she was launched and christened *Dreadnought* on 10 February 1906. Amid a fanfare of publicity she was credited with completion on 3 October, 366 days after keel-laying but these were only 'basin trials' and the *Dreadnought* was not actually ready to go to sea until December. The results were a great credit to the designers and the builders for the turbines gave virtually no trouble and the hull suffered no ill effects from the concussion of such a large number of guns.

The *Dreadnought* put the naval world in a ferment. Although only a logical response to tactical and technical pressures she was immediately seen as a ship which must be copied. The German *Marineamt* was taken completely unawares by her speed of construction and the massive jump in fighting power, and ordered a halt to battleship construction to give their designers time to absorb the new ideas. In the prevailing Anglo-

German tension the newspapers proclaimed that henceforward all comparisons of naval strength must be in 'dreadnoughts' as the 'pre-dreadnoughts' had been made obsolescent. This was nonsense, for the *Dreadnought* was simply a more efficient battleship and would in some circumstances have been at a disadvantage if faced by two smaller ships. But in the age of rampant 'navalism' the British Navy League and the German *Flottenverein* did not bother their heads with such hair-splitting. Nevertheless the arms race between Britain and Germany was given a tremendous fillip, for instead of the Royal Navy's 40 older battleships ranged against 20 German ships of smaller size and weaker armament there was now a margin of only one.

Fisher's Committee on Designs also had to consider the design of a new armored cruiser. As soon as the broad outlines of the *Dreadnought* were settled the Committee started to examine sketch designs but this was like no cruiser yet seen, with 12-inch guns in place of the 9.2-inch carried by the previous *Minotaur*

Class. The design chosen bore a strong resemblance to the *Dreadnought* but had nearly double the horsepower to provide 25 knots. Even so this massive increase in power was only possible because the armor-scale was to be the same as the *Minotaur*'s 6-inch side armor, and only four twin 12-inch turrets were to be mounted instead of five. These were the new 'dreadnought armored cruisers' *Invincible*, *Inflexible* and *Indomitable*, destined to provoke even more controversy than HMS *Dreadnought*. On a displacement of nearly 17,000 tons and armed with eight 12-inch guns there was a natural tendency to equate them with battleships and they were soon unofficially dubbed 'battleship cruisers' and finally in 1912 'battlecruisers.'

The problem was that their proper role was never worked out. Internally they showed very little difference from the *Minotaur* Class, and they were in no sense fast battleships. But Fisher had been greatly impressed by the success of the Japanese armored cruisers at Tsushima and wanted ships which could reconnoiter

Above: The *Nassau* Class dreadnought *Westfalen*.

for the battle fleet, pushing past any small cruisers which tried to stand in their way. For this purpose the 12-inch guns made sense as they would allow the big cruiser to get close enough to the enemy battle-line to count numbers and estimate course and speed. Such a ship could not be dealt with easily by small cruisers and in the closing stages of a fleet action would also be able to swoop on crippled battleships. So far so good, but in the second role of the armored cruiser, protection of commerce, the 12-inch guns were far too big and slow-firing to be of use against small fast moving targets. The new type was therefore a big and expensive solution to that problem. Fisher maintained that the *Invincible* was fast enough to catch anything smaller or escape from anything more powerful, but this presupposed that no other navy had similar ships.

The real weakness of the battlecruiser was that its heavy armament lent it a spurious 'capital' rank, and an admiral would always be tempted to use it to reinforce his battleships. In fact

within a year or two of their completion the term 'capital ship' was introduced to cover both battleships and battlecruisers. The wide disparity between the Russian and Japanese fleets at Tsushima was overlooked, and nobody seems to have thought of what might have happened to Admiral Kamimura's armored cruisers if they had been opposed by a better trained enemy. A ship with a 6-inch armor belt would be vulnerable if she attempted to fight a modern battleship on equal terms, but Fisher airily dismissed this question by saying that 'Speed is Armor.' In one sense that dictum was perfectly valid, but only if the battlecruiser used her superior speed to stay out of trouble. A fast battleship would have been the ideal means of gaining a tactical advantage in battle but a 25-knot ship protected with 12-inch armor would have had to be 50 per cent bigger, and this was not politically or financially acceptable.

Above, above left and below: Four views of the *Dreadnought* under construction. Far left, 2 October 1905, some keel plates and frames already in position. Above left, 28 October, less than one month later, the armored deck being laid. Above, 11 August 1906, nearly complete. Below, mid-February 1906, shortly after launch with funnels but no turrets.

32 .

The Germans replied to both the *Dreadnought* and the *Invincible*, the former with the 20,000-ton *Nassau* Class and the latter with the 19,000-ton *Von der Tann*. The battleships were not an outstanding design, quite well protected but carrying their six 11-inch guns in a cramped arrangement of centerline and wing turrets. The new battlecruisers were a major improvement over the *Invincible*, with good protection and layout. The German designers got closer to the ideal of the fast battleship because they were prepared to sacrifice some speed and gunpower to provide more armor; the 11-inch gun was retained to allow 8-inch armor and the extra tonnage was used to provide better protection against torpedoes.

The British relied on their superior shipbuilding capacity to increase their lead over the Germans, and deliberately made no major alterations to the succeeding classes of dreadnoughts in order to avoid delays. In this way they had seven dreadnoughts of nearly identical design in service by early 1910, *Dreadnought* herself, three *Bellerophon* Class and three *St Vincent* Class, as well as three *Invincible* Class battlecruisers. In the same period

Below right: The stokehold of a British dreadnought. Normally it would be crowded with stokers sweating to feed the fireboxes.
Below: The *Thüringen* of the German *Helgoland* Class. Built 1908–12, this class carried twelve 12-inch guns.

the German Navy commissioned four *Nassau* Class and the *Von der Tann* was still completing. Even the next three British dreadnoughts, the *Neptune* and the two *Colossus* Class and the three *Indefatigable* Class battlecruisers were very similar to their prototypes apart from a modified layout of guns to improve their arcs of fire. In their second class of dreadnoughts, the *Helgoland* Class the Germans decided to adopt a 12-inch gun to match the British gunpower but the British had already decided to put a 13.5-inch gun into the *Orion* Class of 1909.

The race was now an open one, with each class of ship intended to match the latest on the other side of the North Sea. It was useless for the diplomats to try to negotiate any 'holiday' to slow down the tempo of this arms race, for the answer was always 'national survival is at stake.' The cost of a dreadnought at £1–£2 million sounds absurdly cheap today, but in modern terms it represents at least 100 times that figure.

The building of dreadnoughts can be equated with the space program in the 1960s and 1970s, in the sense that it fuelled a crucial area of economic growth and demanded the very best

of contemporary technology, and was also inextricably linked with national prestige. A battleship provided work in the ship-yards and in the steelworks and gun foundries of the nation. Heavy engineering was still the motor force of industrial ex-pansion and the battleship's needs for better armor plate, shells, guns and machinery all stretched various sciences to the limit.

The last chance to effect a reconciliation between German and British interests probably came in 1908. The architect of German naval expansion, Admiral Tirpitz, had successfully fought for his Navy Laws back in the 1890s, legislation which provided for regular replacement of obsolete tonnage instead of the annual haggling between the Navy and Treasury and Parliament, such as went on in Britain. In this Tirpitz was only doing his duty towards his country, to prevent later governments from ham-stringing a long-term program by neglect or sudden whims. But by 1908 the small ineffective coast defense ships had been replaced by ocean-going battleships clearly capable of fighting their opposite numbers in the Royal Navy, and the British did not like the implications. In 1908 Tirpitz used a loophole in the current Navy Law to make a major increase in strength to the German Navy; a provision for replacing eight *grosse Kreuzer* (large or armored cruisers) was interpreted as permitting the building of eight battlecruisers. Although the precedent had been established when Fisher referred to the *Invincibles* as 'dreadnought armored cruisers,' the German move came at a time when German naval expansion was under particularly close scrutiny in Britain. The Liberal government was under strong pressure from its Radical wing to reduce 'bloated arma-ments' but equally torn by fear of losing popular support if it allowed the Royal Navy to be overtaken by the German Navy as a result of unilateral disarmament. There was also the fear of industrial unrest if the tempo of construction should slacken. In Germany too, the situation was not straightforward as the military hierarchy was constantly worried by the threat of a Socialist majority in the Reichstag.

The *Dreadnought* did not cause the First World War but she and her successors were an integral part of the last decade of the old order that passed away in 1914. They were only a symptom of the fever in the veins of Europe, not the fever itself, but there can be no doubt that the endless comparisons of strength and the forecasts of future trends inflamed public opinion and played on deep-rooted fears. The British navalists' slogan, 'We Want Eight and We Won't Wait' expressed the fears and hopes of xenophobes in all the major maritime nations.

READY FOR WAR

The outbreak of war in August 1914 came as something of an anti-climax to the vast fleets which both sides had created. The Germans lay secure behind thick minefields and the guns of the Heligoland fortress while the British battle squadrons had been sent to a pre-arranged rendezvous in the Orkneys, the huge natural harbor of Scapa Flow.

Moving the Home Fleet, given a more ancient and resounding name, the Grand Fleet, on the outbreak of war from its peacetime southern bases to Scapa Flow was a mighty task of logistics and planning. Fortunately July 1914 had seen an experimental full mobilization of the whole fleet to test the arrangements for calling up reservists, and when the First Lord of the Admiralty, Winston Churchill, prudently cancelled leave because of the crisis following the Sarajevo murders virtually the whole strength of the Royal Navy in home waters was ready and fully armed.

Although the British showed none of the recklessness which German plans had counted on, the first use of their capital ships was a piece of opportunism which amply justified the risks taken. On 28 August 1914 a force of light cruisers and destroyers pushed into the Heligoland Bight to attack the German outposts, and ran into stiff opposition from light cruisers. Vice-Admiral Sir David Beatty and four battlecruisers were outside the Bight waiting to cover the withdrawal, but when he heard that the British forces were likely to be overwhelmed he took the *Lion*, *Tiger*, *Queen Mary* and *Princess Royal* in at high speed, ignoring the threat from U-Boats and minefields. The arrival of these powerful ships brought the action to a dramatic end when their 13.5-inch guns sank the light cruisers, *Ariadne* and *Köln*, turning the tables on the Germans and extricating the British light cruisers and destroyers.

In the Mediterranean things went badly, when, by a series of misunderstandings, the German battlecruiser *Goeben* escaped from two of the Mediterranean Fleet's battlecruisers, the *Indomitable* and *Indefatigable*. The *Goeben* and her escorting light cruiser *Breslau* eluded their pursuers and their arrival at the Dardanelles helped to force Turkey from her uneasy neutrality into the arms of the Central Powers. The sinking of Rear-Admiral Cradock's two old armored cruisers off Coronel by a

German squadron under Vice-Admiral Spee on 1 November 1914 led to a swift counterstroke. Three days later Vice-Admiral Sturdee hoisted his flag in the battlecruiser *Invincible* and she and her sister *Inflexible* left Cromarty Firth to go south to Devonport to take on stores. After only a week the two battlecruisers left for South America, arriving at Port Stanley in the Falkland Islands on 7 December. There they found the old battleship *Canopus* and a scratch force of cruisers under Rear-Admiral Stoddart.

The two big ships immediately started the arduous task of coaling and next morning, while they were still engaged on the task, lookouts sighted two German cruisers approaching Port Stanley. The *Canopus* had been put aground on a mud flat to provide a steady gun-platform and soon she was able to open fire to deter the attackers from any attempt to pick off the British ships as they left the harbor. Once the battlecruisers worked their way clear of the harbor the fate of the German squadron was sealed. It was the job for which the battlecruisers had been designed, and as the armored cruisers *Scharnhorst* and *Gneisenau* had not been docked for some time they were bound to be overtaken sooner or later. Sturdee knew this and settled down to a long stern chase, the two battlecruisers belching clouds of coal smoke as they worked up to full speed. Shortly before 1300 the first shots were fired at 16,000 yards. Spee gallantly hauled his flagship and her consort around to give battle and at the same time cover the flight of his three light cruisers, but with four British cruisers in company their freedom would be short-

Above: The old French battleship *Charlemagne* served in the Dardanelles campaign, and for the rest of the war in the Mediterranean.
Above left: Polishing the guns on a German dreadnought.

lived. As the range came down the shooting steadied, and even though both battlecruisers were hit by German shells of all calibers they suffered only slight damage. Both *Scharnhorst* and *Gneisenau* sank after a hopelessly one-sided fight.

Meanwhile the Grand Fleet was learning to live with the soul-destroying routine of life at Scapa Flow. On October 1914 there was a submarine scare in the Flow itself when one of the patrolling destroyers thought she sighted a periscope. Immediately the C-in-C Admiral Sir John Jellicoe ordered the Grand Fleet to be dispersed to a series of temporary bases in Northern Ireland and the west coast of Scotland until permanent net defences and minefields could be provided. For an anxious month the exit to the Atlantic was unguarded but the High Seas Fleet was not inclined to take advantage. Instead Admiral Hipper was instructed to lead his battlecruisers on a raid across the North Sea to bombard Yarmouth in November 1914, followed by a similar bombardment of the Yorkshire coast the following month. The idea behind these pinprick raids was to force the British to divide their fleet and so permit the High Seas Fleet to pounce on a weaker portion of it and fight at favorable odds. It worked, but only partially, to the extent that public outcry forced the Admiralty to move Beatty's battlecruisers from Scapa Flow to Rosyth, where they were better placed to intercept such raids.

Intelligence of a similar raid led the Admiralty to order the Grand Fleet battleships and the Rosyth battlecruisers to meet off the Dogger Bank. This time a light cruiser sighted Hipper's battlecruisers and the result was the brief skirmish known as the Battle of the Dogger Bank, on 24 January 1915. In a hectic stern-chase the flagship *Lion*, the *Tiger*, *Princess Royal*, *New Zealand* and *Indomitable* slowly overhauled Hipper's flagship *Seydlitz*, the *Moltke* and *Derfflinger* and the armored cruiser *Blücher*. The full weight of British fire disabled the *Blücher* bringing up the rear but as a result of a signalling error the British ships halted the chase to concentrate on the sinking *Blücher* although the other German ships were being caught at that time.

The mix-up came at the moment when the *Lion* was badly hit by German gunfire. In all she was hit by 17 shells, one of which burst on the waterline and caused extensive flooding. Although this was brought under control the ship listed to port and slowed down, until finally all light and power failed, bringing the ship to a dead stop. Beatty transferred his flag as quickly as he could but by the time he had resumed control of the action Hipper's

Above: Predreadnoughts of the US Atlantic Fleet in 1917.
Below: The German battlecruiser *Lützow*.

Above: A fine view of the French predreadnought *Saint Louis* showing the pronounced tumble-home favored by French designers. *Saint Louis* served at the Dardanelles.
Below: The *Suffren* (completed 1903) was heavily damaged in March 1915 by Turkish gunfire and sunk in November 1916 by a U-Boat.

ships were drawing out of range and it was hopeless to continue the pursuit. The *Indomitable* took the crippled *Lion* in tow and the whole force returned to Rosyth. The *Blücher* had been sunk but a magnificent opportunity had been wasted.

The adventures of the *Goeben* merit a book to themselves. She had propelled a reluctant Turkey into war with Russia by bombarding Sevastopol at the end of October 1914, despite being nominally Turkish-manned as the *Yawuz Sultan e Selim*. On 18 November she fought a brief action against the Black Sea Fleet, hitting the *Evstafi* four times and receiving one hit in return before escaping in fog. Then on 26 December 1914 she struck two Russian mines off the Bosphorus and this damage prevented her from playing a more prominent part in fending off the Allied attacks in March 1915. On 10 May she met the Black Sea Fleet again, and this time the Russians did much better. The *Evstafi* hit the *Goeben* three times at the creditable range of 16,000–17,500 yards. On 8 January 1916 she met the new dreadnought *Imperatritsa Ekaterina* and was considerably

discomforted to find that the Russian 12-inch guns could elevate to 25 degrees and range out to 28,000 yards.

Shortage of coal kept the *Goeben* in harbor from October 1916 so that she could not take advantage of the declining morale of the Russian Fleet. Not until 20 January 1918 did she venture forth again, this time to strike at the British forces guarding the exit to the Dardanelles. At Imbros she disposed of the monitors *Raglan* and *M.28* with little difficulty but when she and the *Breslau* headed for Mudros both ships struck mines. For the *Goeben* it was the second mine, for she had been slightly damaged by one just after leaving the Dardanelles, but then *Breslau* struck four more and sank. The *Goeben* tried to re-enter the Straits but struck a third mine. She was now being bombed from the air by British aircraft and in the confusion she ran aground off Nagara Point at 15 knots. There she lay for six days while more bombing raids were made on her until finally the old battleship *Torgud Reis* and two tugs came down the Straits to get her afloat again. The bombs were too light to inflict any damage but the mine damage was not fully repaired until long after the war, and she was effectively put out of action until the Armistice.

When the Allies became involved in Greek affairs in 1916 the battleships were withdrawn to Salonika and subsequently four British pre-dreadnoughts were sent to bolster the Italian Fleet at Taranto. The Italians, uneasy at having parity with the Austro-Hungarian Fleet, demanded dreadnoughts but the War Council treated this request with some acerbity. Italians made good use of their ships for shore bombardment in the Northern Adriatic and pushed ahead with the development of motor torpedo boats. On the night of 9–10 December 1917 Captain Luigi Rizzo took *MAS.9* and *MAS.13* into Muggia Bay near Trieste to attack the old battleships *Wien* and *Budapest*. The two 18-inch torpedoes from *MAS.9* struck the *Wien* amidships and she sank quickly but the two fired by *MAS.13* missed the *Budapest* and hit a jetty.

Rizzo scored another outstanding success when in broad daylight on 10 June 1918 his *MAS.15* attacked the dreadnought *Szent Istvan*. The battleship was in company with her sisters about ten miles west of Premuda Island when *MAS.15* and *MAS.21* approached unobserved and fired four torpedoes. The fate of the *Szent Istvan* is well known for as she rolled over she was filmed from another ship, and as the only World War I action movie of a ship sinking it features in many film libraries around the world. The Italian main fleet achieved very little but the efforts of Luigi Rizzo showed that given the right conditions and a vital element of daring the battleship was just as vulnerable as the torpedo boat specialists had prophesied 30 years earlier.

LINE OF BATTLE

Jutland, or Skagerrak to the Germans, remains one of the most fascinating sea battles of all time. The reason is that the result was a baffling paradox; the Germans scored more material successes and cheated the British of a crushing victory, and yet it did them no good whatsoever. Jutland was the first major clash of fleets in European waters since Lissa and the only full-scale battle between the two fleets in the entire war. It was also the largest sea-battle to date, with 252 ships engaged, and the last one in which all the classic ship-types played their parts, battleships, battlecruisers, armored cruisers, light cruisers and destroyers. Ironically it was also the first battle in which aerial reconnaissance played any sort of role.

The two sides had shadow-boxed in the North Sea since August 1914 largely because the German high command was only prepared to sanction hit-and-run raids on the east coast of England. But there was a faction inside the German Navy which wanted a more positive policy and when in February 1916 Vice-Admiral Reinhard Scheer was appointed to command the High Seas Fleet he brought with him a new offensive spirit. This time he planned a coordinated trap for the Grand Fleet, sending U-Boats to mine the exit routes from Scapa Flow and Rosyth and then sending Hipper's First Scouting Group to lure Beatty's battlecruisers into the grip of the whole High Seas Fleet. It might have worked but for the fact that since the end of 1914 the Admiralty had been reading the majority of German cipher messages and when it was realized in London that the High Seas Fleet would be at sea Admiral Jellicoe was ordered to take the Grand Fleet out and rendezvous with Beatty's battlecruisers off the Skagerrak. The composition of the two forces was slightly different from usual because three of Beatty's older battlecruisers had been sent north to Scapa Flow for gunnery practice, and to strengthen the Battlecruiser Fleet it was given four of the *Queen Elizabeth* Class fast battleships.

Everything still depended on chance, but when on 31 May two groups of light cruisers turned to investigate a Danish steamer blowing off steam it was the prelude to a major action. The light cruisers were attached to their respective battlecruisers and each admiral closed the range eagerly in the belief that he could lure the enemy into the arms of his Commander in Chief. Fire was opened at over 24,000 yards, with six British battlecruisers against five German, for in his haste to get into action Beatty had left his 5th Battle Squadron of *Queen Elizabeths* behind. They had deliberately been stationed ten miles astern because Beatty did not want Hipper to refuse action in the face of greatly superior odds but it meant that these four powerful ships were late in coming into action.

The sea was calm but visibility was hazy when the first salvoes thundered out. Beatty had turned east to put himself between Hipper and the German bases while Hipper had turned southeast to draw Beatty back on the High Seas Fleet. Beatty's move was strategically sound but it put him at a disadvantage for the sun was sinking behind his ships, silhouetting them clearly while leaving the German ships merging into the haze. To make matters worse dense clouds of coal smoke and cordite fumes began to roll across the water, adding to the difficulty of reading signals. By an error in signals from the flagship the British ships found themselves firing at the same target while the weakest ship, HMS *Indefatigable* was unsupported in a duel with the *Von der Tann*.

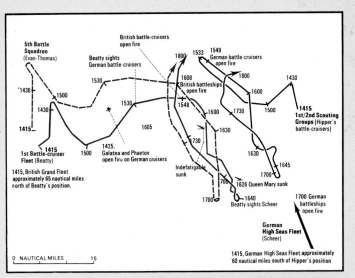

Above: HMS *Indefatigable* seen minutes before she blew up.
Right: Chart of the first phase of the Battle of Jutland.
Bottom: A hurried snapshot taken from HMS *New Zealand* shows the remains of the *Indefatigable* sinking.
Below: SMS *Von der Tann*, the first German battlecruiser, was clearly superior to contemporary British designs.

The action developed rapidly, with the *Moltke* scoring two hits on the *Tiger*, *Derfflinger* finding the range of the *Princess Royal* and the *Lutzow* hitting the *Lion*. At the rear of the line the *Von der Tann* and *Indefatigable*'s fierce duel reached a climax at about 1600 when the German ship scored three hits aft. The British battlecruiser lurched out of the line with smoke pouring from her and sinking by the stern but before she could indicate the extent of her damage another hit landed near the forward 12-inch turret and another hit the turret itself. Suddenly she blew up in a tremendous cloud of brown smoke and sheets of orange flame as her magazines detonated, and when the shower of debris cleared the *Indefatigable* had disappeared with nearly all hands. In only twenty minutes Hipper's ships had evened the odds.

Worse was very soon to follow. The *Derfflinger* shifted fire from the *Lion* to the *Queen Mary* and quickly straddled her. A 12-inch shell hit 'Q' turret amidships and put the right-hand gun out of action and about five minutes later another two shells hit, one near 'A' and 'B' turrets and the other on 'Q' turret. Once again there was a huge explosion as the forepart of the *Queen Mary* vanished in a sheet of flame and smoke. Horrified onlookers saw the remains of the ship listing to port and sinking with the propellers still revolving, and then another explosion obliterated her. Nine men survived out of 1285.

Some clue to the cause of the disaster was gleaned from the experience of the *Lion*. She was hit on 'Q' turret just above the left-hand gun port by a shell which burst above the gun and killed or wounded all the gun crew. A fire broke out among the cordite charges near the guns but a fire party quickly ran a hose over the face of the turret and soused the wrecked turret with water. Yet a full 28 minutes after this the cordite in the turret burst into flame again and spread to the working chamber below. The combustion of the eight full cordite charges was so violent that 'Q' magazine bulkheads were buckled and a venting plate blew out, allowing flames to enter the magazine. Fortunately the magazine had already been flooded by a gallant Royal Marine turret-officer, for if the magazine crew had merely closed the doors they would not have remained flash-tight. When the ship was examined later the burn marks in the hoist showed that the flame had jumped 60 feet, grim proof of how badly unstable cordite could behave.

Help was at hand for the hard-pressed British battlecruisers, however, for the 5th Battle Squadron had caught up and was now able to open fire at extreme range. Within six minutes the flagship *Barham* was hitting the *Seydlitz* at nearly 19,000 yards and HMS *Valiant* was ranging on the *Moltke*. The German ships could not reply at this colossal range, and the only remedy was to make small shifts in course to throw off the British range-takers but this had little effect. To make matters worse Beatty's destroyers launched a torpedo-attack and hit the *Seydlitz*, tearing a huge hole in her side. Yet such was the stout construc-

tion of German battlecruisers that she was able to keep up full speed for a while.

The situation changed dramatically when Beatty learned from his light cruisers that battleships had been sighted and two minutes later he saw for himself the mass of masts, funnels and smoke of the High Seas Fleet. This was just the way it was meant to happen, and he ordered his ships to turn about and go north, secure in the knowledge that the Grand Fleet was hurrying south at top speed to meet him. Yet again, however, the flagship's signal staff were too hasty and omitted to pass on the fresh instructions to the 5th Battle Squadron, leaving them to carry on firing at the German ships until they noticed Beatty's ships turning away. By the time they could be pulled around they were within range of the German battle line and suffered concentrated fire from Hipper's ships as well as the head of Scheer's line. The *Barham* and *Malaya* took several hits and suffered casualties but they and their sisters *Valiant* and *Warspite* fought back and avoided serious damage.

Relief for Beatty's hard-pressed ships was, however, almost at hand for Jellicoe had ordered the 3rd Battle Cruiser Squadron under Rear-Admiral Hood to hurry ahead of the main fleet to reinforce Beatty. The three ships, *Invincible*, *Indomitable* and *Inflexible* came into action just as Beatty was starting to turn to the east across Hipper's bows in a deliberate attempt to prevent him from sighting the Grand Fleet too soon. Now the visibility favored the British for the first time and in order to take the pressure off, Hipper ordered his destroyers to attack the British capital ships. But just as the light craft started to deploy Hood's three battlecruisers appeared out of the haze, 12-inch guns firing. Hood handled his big ships with great skill and within minutes they had inflicted crippling hits on the *Lützow*, reduced the light cruiser *Wiesbaden* to a wreck and damaged the *Pillau* seriously.

It must be remembered that it was now evening and in the worsening visibility the rival commanders were working by guesswork and intuition. For Jellicoe in the Fleet Flagship *Iron Duke* the most urgent problem was to know just *where* the High Seas Fleet would be when it was sighted, and in which direction it would be steaming. From the flag-bridge he could see only seven miles, and if his own fleet was caught in the wrong formation or heading in the wrong direction his superiority in numbers and gunpower would be thrown away. The Grand Fleet was cruising in six columns 'line abreast', a box formation to reduce the risk from submarine attack, and it had to deploy into 'line ahead' to bring every available gun into action. Finally the fog of conflicting and garbled sighting reports resolved itself, the diminutive admiral studied the plot for no more than ten seconds and then gave series of orders for deployment on his port column. It was the right decision for at one stroke he interposed his fleet between the High Seas Fleet and its bases and had brought his most powerful squadrons into action first.

Far right, top: The *Royal Oak* (left) and *Hercules* of the 1st Battle Squadron after the British deployed.
Far right: HMS *Iron Duke*, Jellicoe's flagship.
Below: The Grand Fleet in cruising formation, nearest the camera are ships of the *Iron Duke* Class.

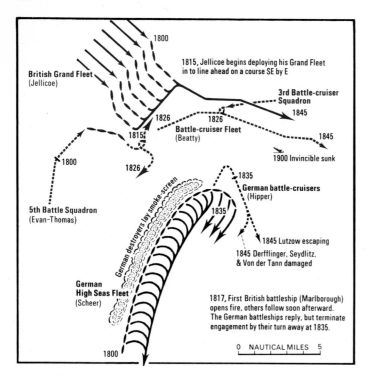

British Grand Fleet
(Jellicoe)

1800

1815, Jellicoe begins deploying his Grand Fleet in to line ahead on a course SE by E

3rd Battle-cruiser Squadron

1845

1826   1826

1815   Battle-cruiser Fleet (Beatty)

1845

1800

1826

1900 Invincible sunk

1835

German battle-cruisers (Hipper)

5th Battle Squadron (Evan-Thomas)

1835

1845 Lutzow escaping

1845 Derfflinger, Seydlitz, & Von der Tann damaged

German destroyers lay smoke-screen

German High Seas Fleet (Scheer)

1817, First British battleship (Marlborough) opens fire, others follow soon afterward. The German battleships reply, but terminate engagement by their turn away at 1835.

1800

0   NAUTICAL MILES   5

Above: The German 'Battle Turn Away.'
Below: HMS *Invincible*'s 'Q' magazine blows up.

As the majestic columns of ships wheeled in turn the two fleets finally sighted one another and ripples of orange flashed down the lines as the first ranging salvoes were fired. Jellicoe had put the Grand Fleet in an ideal position, crossing Scheer's 'T' and concentrating fire on the head of the German line. The British battlecruisers and the *Queen Elizabeths* also appeared out of the murk and took up their allotted position at the ends

of the battle line but during this phase a sudden shift in visibility left the *Invincible* silhouetted against the setting sun, a perfect target for the *Derfflinger* and *Lützow*. At 10,500 yards she was an easy target and was hit five times. The fifth hit blew the roof off 'Q' turret, and once again those ominous clouds of cordite smoke and coal dust billowed up as the *Invincible* broke in two.

In direct contrast to the brilliant performance of Hood's 3rd Battle Cruiser Squadron the armored cruisers of the 1st Cruiser Squadron now immolated themselves in a totally pointless attack. Passing down the engaged side of the battle line and incidentally masking its fire with dense clouds of smoke, Sir Robert Arbuthnot led the *Defence* and three others in a headlong attack on the disabled light cruiser *Wiesbaden*. He paid for his stupidity with his life as the *Defence* blew up while the *Warrior* was reduced to a sinking condition, all to achieve a few hits on a ship which was already sinking. The *Warrior* and the other two were only saved from a similar fate by the arrival on the scene of the battleship *Warspite*, of the 5th Battle Squadron. She and her squadron were trying to follow Beatty's battle-cruisers in taking the place at the end of the line but at a crucial moment her steering jammed, causing her to turn a complete circle near the *Warrior*. The German battleships at the head of the line could not resist the chance of sinking a superdread-nought and immediately switched fire from the cruiser. While the *Warspite*'s people struggled to cool down her overheated steering machinery she continued to circle, surrounded by shell-splashes. The scene was nicknamed 'Windy Corner' by onlookers who were certain that she would be sunk, but in fact she escaped serious damage and was able to get under control again. The distraction also gave the *Warrior* time to crawl away to safety, although she later sank.

The battle was now between the Grand Fleet and the High Seas Fleet, and the German gamble had failed. Jellicoe's in-sistence on constant gunnery practice showed in his flagship's shooting against the *König*. The German ship's diary shows that the *Iron Duke* fired nine salvoes in less than five minutes, of which seven shells hit. One Common shell pierced the lower

edge of the main belt armor and set fire to a number of 5.9-inch charges in a magazine. As with most German cordite it did not explode, in marked contrast to the behavior of British cordite. The loss of the *Indefatigable*, *Queen Mary* and *Invincible* might never have occurred if British propellant had been of the same standard.

The High Seas Fleet had only one course left, its 'Battle Turn Away,' in which all ships turned 180 degrees simultaneously and steamed back on a reciprocal course. It achieved its aim of breaking contact but Jellicoe hauled his Grand Fleet around to the south-east and again to the south twelve minutes later to keep it between the High Seas Fleet and its escape route. At 1908 Scheer blundered into the same trap and this time his position was desperate, with the horizon apparently filled with hostile battleships. He ordered Hipper's battlecruisers on a 'death ride' supported only by the destroyers, to give the main fleet time to make another Battle Turn Away. The destroyers were very roughly handled and the battlecruisers took terrible punishment. The *Lützow* was hit five times and had two turrets out of action; five 15-inch hits on the *Derfflinger* disabled two turrets and started ammunition fires. Three hits on the *Grosser Kurfurst* caused severe flooding. By now the German ships could hardly see the enemy, and the only hits scored were two by the *Seydlitz* on the *Colossus*, which caused minor damage.

The breakaway was successful and the two fleets drew apart for the last time but there was to be one more engagement between heavy ships. Beatty's battlecruisers fired briefly at portions of the High Seas Fleet but at such long range as to be relatively ineffective.

Up to this point Jellicoe could be assured of a handsome victory, for his fleet had proved superior in gunpower and tactics to Scheer's. The loss of life in the *Defence* and the three battlecruisers was tragic but the loss of the four ships had not affected the relative position. Twice the High Seas Fleet had been forced to turn away from the Grand Fleet's guns and still the British were firmly in position across the route back to the German bases. Jellicoe's plan was to station his destroyers well astern of the

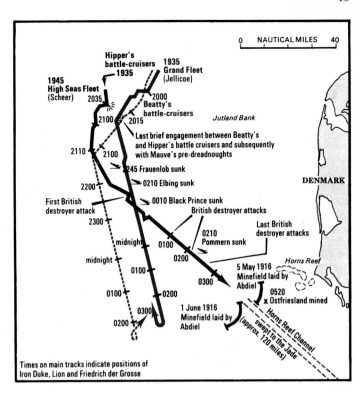

Above: The night action and the German escape.

battle fleet to prevent any attempt by Scheer to double back, and to maintain a cruising formation until daylight, when he hoped to continue the destruction of the High Seas Fleet. British tactics did not favor night action, for the very sound reason that it was a risky business, but they failed to take account of the Germans' absolute necessity to fight at night in order to

escape an annihilating battle in the morning. Furthermore the German Navy had trained for night action whereas the British had not, with the result that when their ships met the British destroyers their reactions were quicker. What also helped was that one of the British battlecruisers had imprudently signalled the correct night challenge and reply to a sister ship, with a German light cruiser watching from the mist. The Germans had only part of the challenge but this was enough to make many British ships hold their fire for fear of hitting a friendly ship.

In spite of these advantages the High Seas Fleet had a frightening ordeal before it finally smashed through the British light forces. When the pre-dreadnought *Pommern* was hit by a single torpedo from HMS *Onslaught* her magazines exploded and she blew up with all hands. The light cruiser *Rostock* was torpedoed and the *Elbing* was rammed by the battleship *Posen* while twisting and turning to avoid torpedoes. The *Lützow* had strained her bulkheads by trying to keep up with the other battlecruisers, and when Scheer learned that she was drawing 70 feet of water forward and was unable to steam he ordered her to be torpedoed.

Once clear of the British flotillas the High Seas Fleet had a clear run home, apart from a mine which damaged the *Ostfriesland*. Although it had performed very creditably it had not won a victory of any sort, except in the sense of avoiding destruction. For the British it was a strategic setback; their fleet had been built at great expense to achieve an overwhelming victory and because that victory eluded them they had to continue with the ruinously expensive war on the Western Front. In relative strength they were hardly affected by the outcome; apart from the *Queen Mary* the losses had been in weak ships and these were replaced very quickly by much more powerful new construction. In the tactical sense they had won; Jellicoe was in possession of the battle area with his fleet intact while Scheer was hurrying back to base as fast as he could. The real blow for the British was to their pride, reputation and confidence. The press and public had been educated to believe that some sort of Trafalgar would happen, a battle of total annihilation, and when the Admiralty unwisely released the text of Scheer's report on the battle because Jellicoe's was not complete, it was construed as proof of a British catastrophe. The losses were impressive but against them could be set the *Lützow* and the *Pommern* and the light cruisers and the virtual sinking of the *Seydlitz* outside Wilhelmshaven. What was alarming was the weakness of training and command, for it soon became apparent that subordinates had rarely shown any initiative in reporting sightings of enemy ships, assuming that the C-in-C already had the information. There had been plenty of gallantry but far too many mistakes and failures to interpret the spirit of the orders as well as the letter.

On the material side the worst shortcoming was undoubtedly the violent behavior of cordite propellant. The root cause of the explosions was that the system for preventing flash from reaching magazines was nowhere near adequate to cope with the unforeseen violence of the flash. Ironically the precautions in British ships were more elaborate than in German ships but because German cordite was more stable it never created an explosion.

A less obvious material failure was the weakness of the British armor-piercing shell, for this meant that the high-quality gunnery of the Grand Fleet during the later phases of the action did much less damage to the German ships than it should have. In all there were 17 hits on German armor varying from 10 to 14 inches in thickness; of these one HE and three glancing Armor-Piercing Capped (APC) had no chance of penetrating, but only one of the remainder penetrated the armor (*Derfflinger*'s barbette) and burst inside. Five more holed the armor without doing more than send fragments through and the other seven shells did not hole the armor. Against lighter armor British shells fared no better, and only one 15-inch APC shell penetrated the *Moltke*'s 8-inch upper belt armor at 18,000 yards.

The cordite and shell problems were tackled energetically by the Admiralty but inevitably it took time for new shells to be manufactured in quantity and for improvements to be made to magazines.

Both fleets completed their repairs as fast as they could but there was to be no second fleet action in the North Sea. The Grand Fleet continued its monotonous sweeps to no avail, but on the one occasion that both fleets were at sea, in August 1916, two of the Grand Fleet's escorting light cruisers were torpedoed and as soon as Scheer learned that Jellicoe was at sea he returned to harbor.

Frustrated and bored the men of the Grand Fleet might be but

Top: A *Queen Elizabeth* Class ship seen during a 'throw-off' gunnery exercise. In such exercises the crew would aim normally at a real target but the equipment would be set to introduce a standard error so that efficiency could be judged safely.
Below: HMS *Superb* (left) and *Canada* seen at Jutland.

ultimately their morale survived intact, whereas that of the High Seas Fleet crumbled. There were two reasons, first the tedium of inactivity in bases never designed to handle such large numbers of men and second, the steady drain of what might be called 'middle management,' the younger officers and qualified petty officers and sailors for service in U-Boats and torpedo boats. The gaps were filled by conscripts and reservists but inevitably the gap between officers and men grew wider and with so little time spent at sea there was plenty of time for grievances to fester. Nor could anyone be unaware of the worsening state of the civilian population as the Allied blockade steadily reduced the quality of foodstuffs. The pressure on the Navy to 'do something' to support their Army comrades fighting in the east and in France was there all the time but as the Grand Fleet was more powerful than it had been before Jutland there was little that Scheer could do without risking a second and more disastrous encounter. The first rumblings of discontent were heard towards the end of 1917 and when at the end of the war Scheer and Hipper tried to take the fleet to sea the sailors mutinied against what they believed to be a suicide mission.

When the end came it was almost unexpected. When the German Army requested an Armistice the British insisted that the High Seas Fleet must be handed over, and this was granted. On 21 November the might of the Grand Fleet mustered off Rosyth to see the unforgettable sight of 14 battleships and battlecruisers steaming in to give themselves up. Between the long lines of ships they went, before being escorted to Scapa Flow for internment until the peace conference at Versailles should decide their fate. Beatty's signal was appropriately curt, 'The German flag will be hauled down at sunset and will not be hoisted again without permission.'

Once at Scapa Flow the German ships were cut off from the outside world, receiving only basic rations and letters from Germany. The British newspaper's available gave very lurid accounts of the progress of negotiations at Versailles, and it was even suggested that the ships should be taken over by the Royal Navy and used to bombard the German coast if the German delegation refused to accept the terms of the peace treaty. Already humiliated by their surrender and aware that the Navy had apparently shown less concern for its professional honor than the Army, the Imperial Navy officers decided on one last token gesture. Taking advantage of the temporary absence of the British battle squadron guarding them, the entire High Seas Fleet scuttled itself at its moorings on 21 June 1919. Boarding parties were able to save only the *Baden* and a few destroyers, but the rest went to the bottom. It marked not only the end of a fleet but the end of the heyday of the battleship. There would be bigger and better ships but never again would the battleship have the unchallenged prestige that she had enjoyed in August 1914.

THE WASHINGTO

Such is the folly of mankind that the victorious Allies of 1918 were embroiled in a new naval arms race within a year. The balance of power was a thing of the past, with the German Navy eliminated and the United States emerging very rapidly as an industrial giant to whom all the other Allies except Japan were heavily in debt. There was only one sane way out, a negotiated mutual reduction of the naval programs, and the United States convened an international naval disarmament conference to meet in Washington in November 1921.

The Washington Conference had far-reaching influence on the development of capital ships. The British accepted that there should be parity with the United States but the Japanese were furious when they were bracketed with the French and

Italians as inferiors of the British and American navies. Both the Japanese and the Americans wanted above all to save what they could out of their huge programs; Japan wanted to avoid scrapping one large battleship while the United States wanted to keep four. All three navies agreed on 16-inch as the maximum gun-caliber, and after some debate 35,000 tons was chosen as the future maximum displacement. Finally the Washington Treaty for the Limitation of Armament was signed in Washington on 13 December 1921.

With a 10-year 'holiday' or moratorium on battleship-building the leading navies turned their minds to modernizing the capital ships left to them under the Treaty. Oil fuel replaced coal and by installing lighter boilers more armor could be used.

Right: The USS *California* seen fitting out at Mare Island Navy Yard in 1920.
Far right, top: The *New Mexico* in dry dock in June 1919. Only US battleships of this vintage featured the clipper bow.
Far right: The British battlecruiser *Hood* was fast and well-armed but was long overdue for a refit to improve her protection when she was sunk by the *Bismarck* in 1941.

N TREATY

Below: In an attempt to reduce the area of heavy armor necessary the *Nelson* and her sister *Rodney* carried all nine of their 16-inch guns forward.

ATLANTIC AND MEDITERRANEAN

When Winston Churchill said, 'We are fighting this war with the ships of the last' he was speaking no more than the truth. Fortunately for the Royal Navy there was no High Seas Fleet across the North Sea, only the nucleus of the big fleet that Admiral Raeder had wanted to build. The British could look forward to a pair of new battleships in 1940–41, whereas the German *Bismarck* was unlikely to be ready until early 1941. Even if Italy came into the war the British hoped that the French fleet would keep the Mediterranean under Allied control.

The British followed the strategy that had proved so successful in World War I, moving the Home Fleet to Scapa Flow to block the exits to the Atlantic, but this time the great fleet base did not prove immune to attack. On the night of 13–14 October 1939 *U.47* under *Kapitänleutnant* Prien penetrated the line of blockships in Kirk Sound and found the old battleship *Royal Oak*

lying at anchor. Prien's salvo of three torpedoes, fired from ahead, failed to do any damage for the one torpedo which hit apparently struck an anchor cable or detonated only partially. After an interval to reload Prien fired another salvo and this time there was a loud explosion underneath the *Royal Oak* and she rolled over and sank 13 minutes later.

As in 1914 the Home Fleet was sent away to bases on the west coast of Scotland until the defenses of Scapa Flow could be strengthened. During this time the *Nelson* was damaged by a magnetic mine while entering Loch Ewe and the *Barham* was hit by a torpedo but the *Kriegsmarine* was not able to take advantage of the Home Fleet's weakness, and it was not until the invasion of Norway in April 1940 that the respective heavy units came into contact. The *Renown* narrowly missed intercepting the German invasion forces on 6 April but three days later in

Above: Jutland veteran HMS *Warspite* served throughout WW2 at Narvik, in the Mediterranean and in support of the D-Day landings.
Below: HMS *Renown* seen in 1940 after a refit. For much of the war she served with Force H at Gibraltar.

Above: The *Littorio* maneuvering under full helm. The ships of this class were fast and graceful and carried nine 15-inch guns. *Littorio* was badly damaged at Taranto. Renamed as the *Italia* she was surrendered to the Allies in 1943.

shocking weather she surprised the battlecruisers *Scharnhorst* and *Gneisenau* some 50 miles from Vestfjord. The British ship's lookouts spotted the Germans through the snow squalls and closed to within nine miles before opening fire. The *Renown* put *Gneisenau*'s forward fire control out of action but she and her sister used their superior speed to get away in the murk. Hitler's orders were quite specific that capital ships were not to expose themselves to damage and so Admiral Lütjens felt obliged to break off the action.

In the second Battle of Narvik the veteran *Warspite* distinguished herself by following a force of nine destroyers up Ofotfjord to hunt down a force of German destroyers. It was hardly an ideal setting for a battleship, with a risk of grounding or being torpedoed but Admiral Whitworth's gamble paid off. Her Swordfish floatplane was able to reconnoiter for the whole

force and her 15-inch guns completed the destruction wrought by the destroyers' guns and torpedoes. At the end of the day the entire German force of eight destroyers had been wiped out, and the *Warspite* had begun a career of extraordinary luck.

Norway showed that air attack was dangerous to battleships. The *Rodney* was damaged and several smaller ships sunk by Ju 87 Stuka dive-bombers and it was at last realised that gunfire alone could not defend ships. Multiple light guns broke up massed attacks and heavier guns could force bombers to keep high but fire control was not yet sufficiently advanced to ensure more than random hits. The vulnerability of aircraft carriers was also demonstrated when during the closing stages of the campaign the *Scharnhorst* and *Gneisenau* caught HMS *Glorious* after she had evacuated the last RAF aircraft and aircrew from Norway. The only opposition came from the destroyer *Acasta*, which managed to hit *Scharnhorst* with a torpedo before being sunk.

The next action involving capital ships was the tragic destruction of the French fleet at Mers-el-Kebir in July 1940. After the fall of France the old battleships *Paris* and *Courbet* had escaped to England and the incomplete *Richelieu* and *Jean Bart* managed to reach North Africa, but four of the remaining capital ships, the *Dunkerque, Strasbourg, Bretagne* and *Provence* had been instructed by the new Pétain Government to remain at Mers-el-Kebir near Oran, under the terms of the Armistice

negotiated with Hitler. The British were understandably alarmed at the collapse of the joint strategy in the Mediterranean, for Italy had chosen this moment to join the war. To guard against any French move the Admiralty immediately formed 'Force H' under Admiral Somerville, including the *Hood*, *Valiant* and *Resolution* and the new carrier *Ark Royal*.

The result was that on 3 July 'Force H' opened fire on the crowded harbor. The 15-inch salvoes quickly overwhelmed the French ships and the *Bretagne* blew up, while the *Dunkerque* and *Provence* were badly damaged. The only large ship to escape the carnage was the *Strasbourg*, which got clear behind the dense clouds of smoke. The *Hood* was only capable of 28 knots and could not catch the French battlecruiser, but Somerville had carried out his orders and the bulk of the French Fleet was now immobilized. But of course as a consequence French opinion was outraged and the French Navy in particular became violently anti-British. Any hopes that individual ships might desert the Vichy cause to join General de Gaulle's Free French Forces in England were dashed. Nor did the failure to take Dakar in September improve relations, for the *Richelieu* was damaged twice by British attacks. This did not stop her from firing on the attacking force with her 15-inch guns, and when HMS *Resolution* was damaged by a torpedo from the submarine *Bévéziers* the attack was cancelled.

For a while it looked as if the powerful Italian Fleet might force the British to abandon the Mediterranean but this gloomy view took no account of the difference in temperament between the British and the Italians. Admiral Cunningham was given the *Warspite* as his flagship and the unmodernized *Royal Sovereign*, *Ramillies* and *Malaya* as well as the old carrier *Eagle*. With this force Cunningham had no hesitation in giving battle to the Italians, and the result of the action off Calabria on 9 July showed that his confidence was justified. Both the Italians and the British were at sea to cover the passage of convoys when Admiral Campioni's squadron was sighted by the British. A torpedo-attack by the *Eagle*'s Swordfish was unsuccessful but the *Warspite* was at extreme gun-range. As the Italian ships worked up to full speed, heading for the horizon, the *Warspite*'s guns fired their first salvoes in anger since Jutland 24 years earlier. Suddenly an orange flash appeared on the flagship *Giulio Cesare* as a 15-inch shell landed alongside her funnels. That was the end of the action for the Italians retired under cover of a smokescreen and used their higher speed to get away. The British were naturally disappointed but the action showed that they had little to fear from the Italian fleet. Incidentally the *Warspite*'s record of a hit at 26,400 yards still stands, the greatest range at which naval guns have scored a hit on a moving target.

The next action, between 'Force H' and Campioni off Cape Spartivento on 27 November was inconclusive but Cunningham had already inflicted a serious defeat on the Italians. With a new carrier, HMS *Illustrious* and another modernized battleship, the *Valiant* he was able to attack the enemy in his main base at Taranto. On the night of 11–12 November a force of 21 Swordfish biplane torpedo-bombers attacked Taranto, sinking the *Conte di Cavour* and severely damaging the new *Littorio* and the *Duilio*. Although the damaged ships would be repaired the attack meant that three out of six battleships were out of action. More important the Italians had lost the initiative to the British, who could now send convoys through the Mediterranean to reinforce their forces in Malta and Egypt. Ever since 1918, when it had been planned to use Sopwith Cuckoo torpedo-bombers to attack the High Seas Fleet, the Fleet Air Arm had hoped for such an opportunity, and now it had made history. Among the interested parties who studied the results of Taranto were the Japanese, who were at that moment thinking of ways to do much the same thing to the Americans at Pearl Harbor.

Early in 1941 Cunningham at last had his chance to strike a blow at the Italian Fleet. On 28 March the carrier *Formidable*'s torpedo-bombers put two torpedoes into the new battleship *Vittorio Veneto*, giving the Mediterranean Fleet a chance to cut

Above: An Italian battleship opens fire during the Battle of Cape Spartivento. The British cruiser *Berwick* was damaged before the Italians broke off the action.
Below: HMS *Nelson* down by the bow after being hit by an Italian aerial torpedo while escorting a Malta convoy.

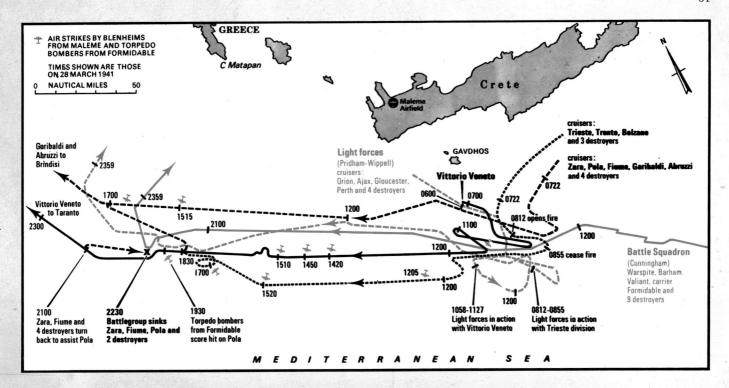

AIR STRIKES BY BLENHEIMS FROM MALEME AND TORPEDO BOMBERS FROM FORMIDABLE

TIMES SHOWN ARE THOSE ON 28 MARCH 1941

0 NAUTICAL MILES 50

GREECE

C Matapan

Crete

Maleme Airfield

GAVDHOS

cruisers: Trieste, Trento, Bolzano and 3 destroyers

cruisers: Zara, Pola, Fiume, Garibaldi, Abruzzi and 4 destroyers

Garibaldi and Abruzzi to Brindisi
2359

Light forces (Pridham-Wippell) cruisers: Orion, Ajax, Gloucester, Perth and 4 destroyers

Vittorio Veneto

Vittorio Veneto to Taranto
2300

2100 Zara, Fiume and 4 destroyers turn back to assist Pola

2230 Battlegroup sinks Zara, Fiume, Pola and 2 destroyers

1930 Torpedo bombers from Formidable score hit on Pola

1058-1127 Light forces in action with Vittorio Veneto

0812-0855 Light forces in action with Trieste division

Battle Squadron (Cunningham) Warspite, Barham, Valiant, carrier Formidable and 9 destroyers

MEDITERRANEAN SEA

Above: Chart of the Battle of Matapan.

her off. At dusk Cunningham's ships were still 65 miles astern but he had already made up his mind to risk a night action and pressed on. Since Jutland the Royal Navy had learned a lot and although only a few ships had radar they were equipped with such aids as flashless cordite and the drills had been practiced endlessly. In contrast the Italians were badly equipped, with no radar but above all lacking any sort of training for night-fighting.

The object of the pursuit, the *Vittorio Veneto* had actually escaped and was heading for home but just before dusk a stray aircraft torpedo had hit one of her escorting cruisers, the *Pola*. Admiral Iachino ordered two of her sisters, the *Fiume* and the *Zara* to go back and try to tow her home. It was while these two ships were looking for their stricken consort that they appeared as echoes on the British radar screens. Suddenly they realized that they had fallen into a trap, but too late.

The Battle of Cape Matapan, or Gaudo Island to the Italians, was a massacre. The *Warspite*, *Barham* and *Valiant* sank the *Fiume* and *Zara* in minutes, despite a gallant attempt by the escorting destroyers to defend them. Then the British destroyers hunted down the crippled *Pola* and torpedoed her after taking off as many survivors as they could.

Cunningham did not regard Matapan as anything more than a skirmish for he had intended to sink the *Vittorio Veneto* but its strategic value came to light two months later. During the evacuation of Crete the Mediterranean Fleet was exposed to merciless dive-bombing and was suffering heavy losses. Now was the time for the Italian Fleet to put to sea but somehow it failed to grasp the opportunity to avenge Matapan. Even after German U-Boats sunk the carrier *Ark Royal* and HMS *Barham* and Italian frogmen had put the *Queen Elizabeth* and *Valiant* out of action in Alexandria, the memory of Matapan continued to inhibit the Italian high command, and they lost their last chance to dominate the Mediterranean.

Back in home waters the British faced a serious threat from the German heavy surface ships. In 1939–40 and again in 1941 the *Scharnhorst* and *Gneisenau* had sortied into the North Atlantic, sinking the armed merchant cruiser HMS *Rawalpindi* and 22 merchant ships totalling over 115,000 tons gross. To counter the threat to the Atlantic convoys the Admiralty reinforced each convoy with an old battleship. Although these veterans were totally outclassed, on the two occasions that the

German ships made contact the sight of a tripod mast and control top was sufficient to make them sheer off. Hitler's orders had to be obeyed, even when they ran counter to common sense.

A much more dangerous threat was the battleship *Bismarck*, which completed her training and shakedown by April 1941. With a margin of 6000 tons over the Washington Treaty limit the designers had been able to produce a balanced design, fast, well-armed and well-protected. When the Admiralty learned of the movement of two large ships westward out of the Baltic it was obvious that the *Bismarck* and the new heavy cruiser *Prinz Eugen* were ready to break out into the Atlantic. On 21 May they sailed from Bergen and disappeared but already two heavy cruisers, HMS *Norfolk* and HMS *Suffolk* were patrolling their most likely exit-route, the Denmark Strait between Iceland and Greenland. As the *Suffolk* was equipped with radar she was able to make contact in spite of the bad visibility on 23 May. The old battlecruiser *Hood* and the new battleship *Prince of Wales* had already sailed from Scapa Flow. They intercepted the German ships shortly after dawn on the 24th.

The action opened briskly with *Hood* firing well on ranges supplied by her Type 284 radar. Her first three salvoes were right for distance but off line, and in the opinion of the *Bismarck*'s surviving 3rd gunnery officer the next salvo looked likely to hit. But instead, just as the *Hood* turned to port to bring her full broadside to bear she vanished in a huge explosion. When the smoke cleared the two halves of the ship could be seen disappearing, just like the battlecruisers at Jutland. Then a tornado of fire burst about the *Prince of Wales* as both *Bismarck* and *Prinz Eugen* concentrated their fire on her. She was hit seven times by four 15-inch and three 8-inch shells, the worst hit being a 15-inch shell which passed through the compass platform without detonating. It scattered fragments of the

Below: The 'pocket battleship' *Graf Spee* on fire after being scuttled in Montevideo harbor. Ships of this type were designed as commerce raiders but were not a success.

binnacle around, killing or wounding everyone except Captain Leach. The *Prince of Wales* fought back gamely coping with a crop of teething troubles as well as the disastrous hit on the compass platform. Straddles were obtained, and it was later learned that two 14-inch shells hit the *Bismarck* below the waterline, a creditable achievement for any new ship.

The Admiralty now mustered all its resources to hunt down the *Bismarck*. The carrier *Ark Royal* and the *Renown* had already left Gibraltar and the battleship *Rodney* left her convoy to join the Home Fleet. The C-in-C Home Fleet, Admiral Tovey was at sea in the *King George V*, heading for the last known position of the German ships, and all available aircraft and ships were searching, for the heavy cruisers *Norfolk* and *Suffolk* had lost radar contact. Late on the night of 24 May the *Bismarck* had been hit by an 18-inch aerial torpedo from one of the *Victorious'* Swordfish but this had exploded on the armor belt amidships and had not slowed her down. What nobody knew was that the two hits from the *Prince of Wales* had damaged the *Bismarck*'s fuel tanks, contaminating a large part of her oil and leaving a long slick.

Finally on 26 May a Catalina flying boat sighted the oil slick and identified the *Bismarck*. She was now heading for Brest in Brittany, for Admiral Lutjens had realized that the Atlantic sortie would be impossible without the full load of fuel. But the nearest British heavy ships would not be able to close the distance before the *Bismarck* came under the shelter of shore-based aircraft. It was essential to slow her down before this happened and so the *Ark Royal* was ordered to fly off a torpedo-strike.

The first wave of Swordfish nearly sank HMS *Sheffield*, one of the Home Fleet cruisers in the area, but the second strike was a success. In spite of withering fire from the guns the Swordfish managed to get two hits, one on the armor and one right aft. The second wrecked the steering gear and jammed the rudders, leaving the giant ship careering helplessly in circles until she could be slowed down and steered on the pro-

Above: The main armament of HMS *Rodney*.

pellers. Throughout the night the *Bismarck*'s crew worked to free the rudders for their lives depended on it. Divers might have gone over the side with explosives to blow the tangled wreckage away but the rough weather put it out of the question.

Early next morning the Home Fleet hove into sight, the flagship *King George V* and the *Rodney* and at 2047 the British fired their first salvoes. The first German salvoes were accurate, straddling the *Rodney* but thereafter *Bismarck*'s gunnery fell off rapidly and within half an hour she was silenced. Admiral Tovey ordered the flagship out to 14,000 yards to get more plunging hits and sent the *Rodney* in to 4000 yards to fire full broadsides at the superstructure but still she would not sink.

By now the battleships were running short of fuel after their long chase and Tovey decided to break off the gun action, leaving the job of sinking the tortured wreck to the torpedoes of the heavy cruiser *Dorsetshire*. Three torpedoes hit the starboard side and then the *Dorsetshire* moved around to fire a fourth into the port side, and at 1036 the *Bismarck* sank.

The sinking of the *Bismarck* put an end to the *Kriegsmarine*'s plans to disrupt Atlantic shipping with surface forces. Thereafter the *Scharnhorst*, *Gneisenau* and *Prinz Eugen* remained at Brest, subjected to heavy if inaccurate high-level bombing by the RAF. Sooner or later they were likely to be hit and so in January 1942 Hitler ordered Naval Group Command West to bring the three ships back to Germany. The plan for Operation Cerberus had all the hallmarks of Hitlerian genius, a daylight dash through the English Channel in the teeth of coastal guns, air attacks and surface ships. Once again Hitler had divined his opponents' weakness: nobody *believed* that heavy units would dare to go through the Channel, and as long as a heavy 'umbrella' of fighters was provided by the Luftwaffe the risk was small. And so it turned out on 12 February 1942 when the three ships managed to get through the Channel unscathed, apart from striking mines at the end of the day.

After her escape the *Scharnhorst* was sent to join the *Tirpitz* and the surviving cruisers and destroyers in Northern Norway, where they could at least threaten the convoys taking supplies to Murmansk. Although the *Tirpitz* played a major part in the destruction of convoy PQ.17 it was merely a false report that she had left harbor which did the damage. For the rest of the time the heavy ships played the part of a 'fleet in being.' When the *Tirpitz* was immobilized by British midget submarines in September 1943 it was left to the *Scharnhorst* to make some sort of effort to stop the convoys getting through. The new Commander in Chief, Dönitz, obtained permission from Hitler to mount a major operation but on condition that Hitler refrained from interfering. Northern Group was commanded temporarily by Admiral Bey, who was under the impression that a destroyer-raid was all that was intended, but at the last minute he was told that the *Scharnhorst* ought to be sent out as well.

With the British reading many of the top-level signals the circumstances were hardly favorable, but on Christmas Day the *Scharnhorst* and five destroyers sailed from Altenfjord. Their objective was a convoy outward bound for Murmansk, for reconnaissance had failed to detect a second convoy, homeward bound from the Kola Inlet to Loch Ewe. The two convoys were escorted by cruisers and destroyers, with a distant escort provided by the battleship *Duke of York*, the cruiser *Jamaica* and four destroyers. The C-in-C Home Fleet, Admiral Fraser, was sufficiently certain of German intentions to transfer some escorts from one convoy to the other strengthening it to 14 destroyers. Admiral Bey was taking his force into a hornet's nest, and when he lost contact with his destroyers early next morning disaster became certain. Unaware that the *Duke of York* and *Jamaica* were only 200 miles away, closing at a steady

17 knots the *Scharnhorst* continued on course to intercept the convoy.

At 0840 the cruiser *Belfast* picked up the *Scharnhorst* on radar at 30 miles, and three-quarters of an hour later she fired star-shell into the Arctic gloom. Then the *Norfolk* opened fire and an 8-inch shell smashed into the *Scharnhorst*'s foretop, destroying the fire control director. Badly shaken, the battlecruiser turned away, her bulk enabling her to outstrip the cruisers in the heavy seas. Admiral Burnett, flying his flag in HMS *Belfast*, ordered the three cruisers to return to the convoy. It was feared for a time that the *Scharnhorst* would return to base but just after mid-day she reappeared and opened fire on the cruisers at 11,000 yards. The *Norfolk* was hit in an 8-inch turret and had most of her radar sets knocked out but the three cruisers fought back and forced the battlecruiser to turn away.

The *Scharnhorst* had unwittingly turned in the direction of the *Duke of York* and at 1617 the Home Fleet flagship picked her up on radar. When the range came down to 12,000 yards the *Duke of York* opened fire, taking the *Scharnhorst* completely by surprise. She sheered away sharply but the duel continued at ranges of 17,000–20,000 yards as she used her speed to open the range. Her gunnery improved but the two hits on the *Duke of York* went through masts without exploding. The *Duke of York*'s gunnery was excellent, and even when the *Scharnhorst* made small alterations of course to avoid the salvoes radar-plotting was able to allow for them. One or more of the 14-inch hits damaged a propeller shaft but this was not enough to cripple the *Scharnhorst* and eventually Admiral Fraser ordered his destroyers to attack. They achieved four hits.

Below: The battleships *Nevada, Texas, Arkansas, Warspite* and *Ramillies* led the D-Day bombardment operations.

The *Duke of York* opened fire again at 10,400 yards and within half an hour the *Scharnhorst*'s speed was down to 5 knots. She was burning furiously and shrouded in smoke and when the *Jamaica* closed in for the *coup de grace* with torpedoes she reported that all she could see was a dull glow in the smoke. Nobody saw the end of *Scharnhorst* at around 1945 and only 36 survivors were found in the icy water. She had gone down with nearly 2000 men on board, a victim of an outdated strategy and poor intelligence.

With the *Scharnhorst* gone it remained only to account for the *Tirpitz* which had survived many attempts to sink her. The problem was basically one of topography, for it was almost suicidal to make a low-level bombing run against a ship moored close to the side of a fjord. On the one occasion that a 750-pound bomb hit it penetrated all the decks but failed to burst. Next the X-Craft attack in September 1943 damaged her machinery and turrets severely. This forced the Germans to move her to a more southerly base for repairs, and once at Kaafjord she was within reach of RAF bombers flying from Northern Russia. On 15 September 1944 a force of 27 Lancasters attacked carrying new weapons, the 12,000-pound 'Tallboy" bomb and 400-pound JWII buoyant bombs. One hit forward caused great damage to the forepart of the ship and two near misses put the machinery out of action.

Time was running out for the Third Reich and the high command decided that the best use for the *Tirpitz* was as a floating fortress to defend Tromsö. With her damaged bow temporarily repaired the *Tirpitz* was moved from Kaafjord to Haakoy Island, three miles west of Tromsö in mid-October. Here she was at last within range of Lancasters flying from the far north of Scotland, and, after an unsuccessful attempt on 29 October, 32 Lancasters attacked with Tallboys on 12 November. The aircraft

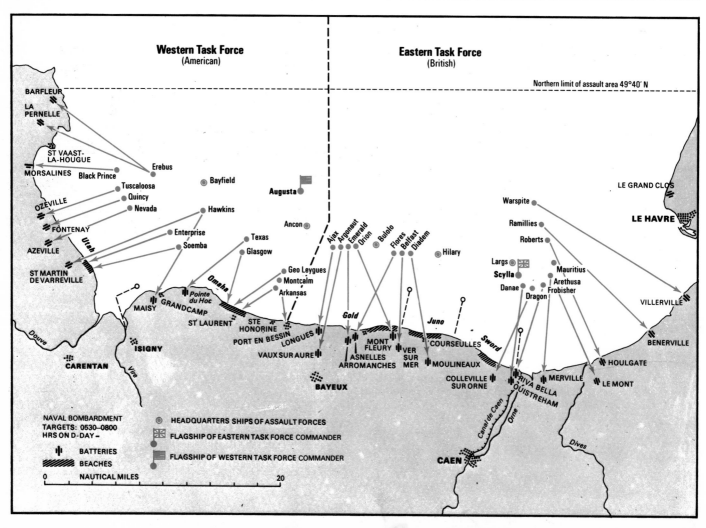

Above: The panzerschiff *Deutschland* was the first of her class to be built. Her name was later changed to *Lützow* on Hitler's orders.

had it all their own way, evading radar cover until they were only 75 miles away and not meeting any defending fighters. In clear weather the bomb-aimers were able to achieve what they had been planning for three years and three hits were observed. Although still firing her antiaircraft guns the *Tirpitz* began to list heavily and ten minutes after the attack had begun she rolled over and sank. It had taken 13 air attacks by 600 air-craft and an attack by midget submarines to finish off the last German capital ship.

The last duty for battleships in the European theatre was to provide covering fire for the big amphibious landings, starting with Torch and ending at Normandy. In June 1944 seven US and British battleships provided fire support for the D-Day landings, blasting concrete emplacements on the Atlantic Wall and disrupting German movements in response to calls from troops ashore. It was the last moment of glory for the older ships such as the USS *Arkansas* and *Nevada* and HMS *Warspite*, no longer able to take their place in the battle line but still capable of accurate shooting. They were only part of the massive effort which went into the liberation of Europe but they symbolized the way in which sea power had been the final deciding factor.

Right: The USS *Texas* is straddled by fire from a German shore battery whole bombarding Cherbourg, 25 June 1944.
Below: The *Littorio* Class *Vittorio Veneto* at speed.

VULNERABLE GIANTS

War in the Pacific had been brewing for many years for as Japan grew in military and industrial power she grew more aware of just how flimsy the Western colonial empire was. But the overriding need for Japan was raw materials, tin, rubber and oil to sustain her economic growth. Apart from coal the Japanese Home Islands lacked most of the important raw materials, and as these existed in abundance in the East Indies it was inevitable that Japanese thoughts should turn to conquest.

Standing in the way of expansion was the United States, and in particular her Pacific Fleet based on Pearl Harbor. The British were fully engaged in fighting the Germans and Italians and so were unable to spare reinforcements but the US Navy would have to be neutralized before any action could be taken in the East Indies. By 1940 the plans were ready for a daring strike to knock out the American Fleet and then occupy a huge defensive perimeter of island bases across the Pacific. Behind this 'island barrier' the Japanese hoped to be able to absorb any counterattacks and reduce enemy strength by attrition from submarines. The British attack on Taranto was studied with great interest, for the Japanese intended to repeat it on a much larger scale, using more modern aircraft in greater numbers.

At the end of November 1941 a fleet of six aircraft carriers, two battleships and three heavy cruisers put to sea for the attack on Pearl Harbor. Avoiding shipping routes the task force was in position 375 miles north of Hawaii by the night of 6–7 December without being detected. At 0700 next morning the first wave of aircraft left the carriers, and only two hours later the raid was over. The impossible had happened; the great base had been taken by surprise and eight battleships had been sunk or badly damaged. Most of the damage had been done by the first wave, for the aircraft were able to identify 'Battleship Row' easily. At 0810 a hit by a 1600-pound bomb on the *Arizona* detonated her forward magazines and she was blown apart. The *Oklahoma* capsized and the *California*, *Maryland*, *Tennessee* and *West Virginia* were badly damaged. The *Nevada* was set on fire and was nearly sunk in the harbor entrance but managed to put herself ashore out of the fairway. The only battleship to escape serious damage was the *Pennsylvania*, but even she required extensive repairs and to all intents and purposes the US Pacific Fleet had been wiped out.

There were a few compensations. The carriers had all been away exercising on the fatal Sunday and in their enthusiasm the Japanese pilots had omitted to destroy the huge tank farms. If the 4.5 million barrels of oil fuel stored there had been destroyed Pearl Harbor would have been finished as a base, no matter how many ships had survived.

The next to feel the weight of Japanese air power were the British, who had finally sent the *Prince of Wales* and the *Repulse* to the Far East at the eleventh hour in the hope that this might intimidate the Japanese. The attack on Pearl Harbor robbed the ships of any strategic value but in any case they were doomed for there was only rudimentary air cover from a few obsolescent RAF fighters. Three days after Pearl Harbor as the two ships were searching for a reported amphibious landing on the east coast of Malaya they were attacked by a mixed force of 30

bombers and 50 torpedo-bombers. The *Repulse* was slightly damaged by a bomb but the *Prince of Wales* was hit aft by a torpedo. Within minutes the ship had taken on some 2500 tons of water in the machinery compartments and was listing $11\frac{1}{2}$ degrees. Then the shock of near-misses knocked out all the electric generators and the antiaircraft mountings lost power. A second wave of attacks missed both ships but the third wave put four more torpedoes into the starboard side. By now the *Prince of Wales* was doomed for her pumps could not cope with the progressive flooding but she could still steam. She made off slowly to the north and survived a further bomb hit at 1244 but at 1320 she suddenly lurched further to port and capsized.

The *Repulse*, despite her age, showed great skill in dodging the attacks but the third attack scored a hit aft. Unable to steer, she was helpless and took three more torpedoes, before capsizing. Destroyers were able to rescue Captain Tennant and 796 crew. It was the end of nearly a century of Western supremacy in the Far East, and also the end of the battleship's supremacy. Even if it could be argued that none of the other ships were modern, the *Prince of Wales* was a new-generation ship designed specifically to survive air attacks.

In retrospect the destruction of the battle fleet at Pearl Harbor was a blessing for it freed the American naval aviators from pre-war concepts of operating carriers as an adjunct to the battle squadrons. Now the fast carrier task group had to be the main striking force because there was no other, and the first big battles in 1942, Coral Sea and Midway, were decided by rival air groups without the surface fleets making contact at all. Particularly at Midway, when the Japanese C-in-C Admiral Yamamoto had seven battleships, including the giant *Yamato* and yet was powerless to defeat three American carriers. In 1942 both sides finally concluded that the battleship was no longer relevant and all work on battleships was downgraded in favor of greatly expanded carrier programs.

Freed from the treaty restrictions the US Navy could now build the ships that it wanted, and in 1939–40 six 45,000-ton *Iowa* Class were authorized, followed by five *Montana* Class displacing 56,000 tons. The *Iowas* were magnificent ships, fast and long-legged to keep up with the carriers. But in the meantime the burden had to be borne by the veterans. With a tremendous effort the Pearl Harbor casualties were repaired, apart from the *Arizona* and *Oklahoma*, some to be sent back into service with only updated antiaircraft batteries and others after total rebuilding.

When US forces landed on Guadalcanal on 7 August 1942 powerful Japanese surface forces were thrown in to try to dislodge them. On the night of 12–13 November 1942 the fast battleships *Hiei* and *Kirishima* attempted to bombard the US Marines' strip at Henderson Field but were surprised by a force of US cruisers and destroyers. In a fierce short-range action the *Portland* and *San Francisco* inflicted severe damage on the *Hiei*, and after she took a probable torpedo-hit she withdrew to the north. Her sister *Kirishima* escaped with only one 8-inch hit but planes from the carrier *Enterprise* found *Hiei* next day and harried her mercilessly. Finally she was abandoned and sunk by her escorting destroyers.

The following night another bombardment was attempted but

Above: The USS *New Mexico* is hit by a suicide plane. Kamikazes damaged *New Mexico* twice, in January and May 1945.
Right: The battleship *Colorado* in 1942. She carried the old-fashioned 'cage' masts until modernized in 1944.

this time the battleships *Washington* and *South Dakota* were in support. At 2316 both battleships opened fire on a Japanese light cruiser, only to suffer the sort of unpleasant surprise the British had suffered at Jutland. The Japanese were experts at night-fighting and they opened fire immediately with guns and torpedoes. All four American destroyers were put out of action before they could fire their own torpedoes, and to add to the confusion the *South Dakota* suddenly went out of control. About 17 minutes after the action had started the concussion from one of her twin 5-inch gun mountings caused a short-circuit in the electrical system. Although the power-loss lasted only three minutes the entire ship was in darkness and there was no power for guns, gyros or fire control. She turned to avoid the blazing destroyers but blundered off towards the Japanese line. At a range of only 5800 yards she was silhouetted against the glow and was fired on by the *Kirishima* and the heavy cruisers *Atago* and *Takao*.

The *South Dakota* was saved from serious damage because the *Washington* had prudently kept her searchlights switched off. Firing on radar the *Washington* was able to close to 8400 yards before riddling the *Kirishima* with nine 16-inch hits. The Americans withdrew to lick their wounds, leaving the Japanese destroyers to save the survivors of the *Kirishima* before sinking her with torpedoes. Although tactically an American victory it had revealed serious weaknesses in their organization.

As the new battleships joined the Fleet the older ships were relegated to bombardment duties in support of the various amphibious landings. The role of the newer fast battleships was

Above: Quadruple 40mm Bofors antiaircraft mountings were fitted to all US battleships from 1942 onward.
Above left: Opening the breech of a 16-inch gun on a US battleship.

not merely to ward off surface attacks on the carriers but to provide additional antiaircraft firepower. Being designed as steady gun-platforms their fire control was better than a cruiser's or a destroyer's, so that their effectiveness 'per barrel' was greater. In the Battle of the Philippine Sea in June 1944 Admiral Willis A Lee's seven fast battleships, were disposed in a battle line 15 miles east of the nearest carriers. Their task was to put up a 'wall of fire' to thin out any Japanese carrier planes trying to attack Admiral Spruance's forces, and this they did superbly, inflicting many casualties.

The last battle of the Pacific was also the biggest in history. The Battle of Leyte Gulf, in reality four separate battles, saw all types of warship functioning as designed; battleships, cruisers and destroyers were all involved in possibly the last conventional surface actions ever fought. The battle came about because the Japanese, in spite of the losses that they had

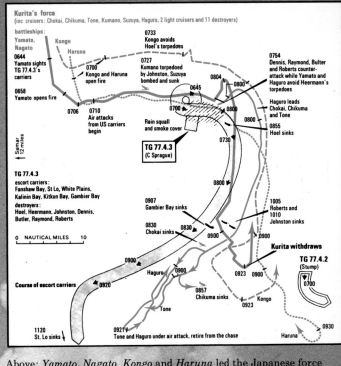

Kurita's force
(inc cruisers: Chokai, Chikuma, Tone, Kumano, Suzuya, Haguro, 2 light cruisers and 11 destroyers)

battleships:
Yamato, Nagato, Kongo, Haruna

0644 Yamato sights TG 77.4.3's carriers

0658 Yamato opens fire

0706

0710 Air attacks from US carriers begin

0700 Kongo and Haruna open fire

0727 Kumano torpedoed by Johnston, Suzuya bombed and sunk

0645

0700

0730

0733 Kongo avoids Hoel's torpedoes

Rain squall and smoke cover

TG 77.4.3 (C Sprague)

0804

0800

0800

0800

0800

0754 Dennis, Raymond, Bulter and Roberts counter-attack while Yamato and Haguro avoid Heermann's torpedoes

Haguro leads Chokai, Chikuma and Tone

0855 Hoel sinks

Samar 12 miles

TG 77.4.3
escort carriers:
Fanshaw Bay, St Lo, White Plains, Kalinin Bay, Kitkun Bay, Gambier Bay
destroyers:
Hoel, Heermann, Johnston, Dennis, Butler, Raymond, Roberts

0907 Gambier Bay sinks

0830 Chokai sinks

0830

0800

0900

0900

1005 Roberts and 1010 Johnston sinks

0 NAUTICAL MILES 10

0900

Haguro

0900

0920

Course of escort carriers

0857 Chikuma sinks

Tone

0900

0923

0900

0923

Kongo

Kurita withdraws

TG 77.4.2 (Stump)

0700

0930

Haruna

1120 St. Lo sinks

0921 Tone and Haguro under air attack, retire from the chase

Above: *Yamato, Nagato, Kongo* and *Haruna* led the Japanese force in the Battle of Samar.
Below: The USS *Missouri* seen soon after she commissioned.

taken since the heady days after Pearl Harbor, still hankered after an annihilating battle between the two fleets. The demolition of their island perimeter and dwindling oil reserves made it imperative to do something decisive, and the invasion of the Marianas in mid-1944 finally forced their hand. It did not take a genius to predict that the next American thrust would be in the Philippines, and to defeat this the *Sho-1* or Victory Plan was conceived. It was to be a final gambler's throw with the entire surface fleet committed to tempt the Americans into a full-scale action. It was crude but simple; without sufficient carrier aircrews to fly from the carriers the surface forces would have to force their way through to the invasion areas. Faced with this threat the Americans would have to bring in their main fleet and give battle.

Command of the Mobile Force was entrusted to Vice-Admiral Ozawa and comprised four carriers and the two hybrid battleship-carriers *Hyuga* and *Ise* (but without aircraft), as well as three cruisers. Vice-Admiral Kurita had Forces 'A' and 'B', the heavy striking force, comprising the 64,000-ton *Yamato* and *Musashi*, the *Nagato*, *Haruna* and *Kongo* and 12 cruisers. Force 'C' was divided into a Van Squadron under Vice-Admiral Nishimura, with *Fuso* and *Yamashiro* and a single heavy cruiser, and a Rear Squadron under Vice-Admiral Shima, with three heavy cruisers. To the Americans these formations were identified by their location: the Mobile Force was labelled the 'Northern Force,' Forces 'A' and 'B' became the 'Center Force' and Force 'C' the 'Southern Force.'

Ozawa's role was that of decoy to draw Admiral Halsey's Fast Carrier Task Force away from the invasion fleet. Forces 'A' and 'B' would then join Force 'C' to destroy the invasion fleet, brushing aside any opposition. Against the 18-inch guns of the *Yamato* and *Musashi* and the fearsome Long Lance torpedoes of the cruisers and destroyers would be ranged only six old battleships, the *Mississippi*, *Maryland*, *West Virginia*, *Tennessee*, *California* and *Pennsylvania* for all the fast battleships were with Halsey's Third Fleet. Decoying Halsey would also reduce the threat from air attack, it was hoped, for the attackers would only be faced by the Seventh Fleet's escort carriers. It was accepted that Ozawa's force would probably be destroyed but, faced with the risk of certain defeat within a few months, the Japanese felt that the sacrifice would be worthwhile.

As soon as the first assault waves were reported moving into Leyte Gulf *Sho-1* was put into action, Ozawa sailing from Japan and Kurita, Nishimura and Shima from Brunei. But things went wrong almost immediately for Kurita's heavy units were sighted by two US submarines as they passed through the Palawan Passage. After sending off the vital news the two submarines made a brilliant attack, torpedoing three heavy cruisers. The Japanese air forces in the Philippines had wasted their strength in largely unsuccessful attacks on American carriers rather than provide a combat air patrol over Kurita's ships and so they now felt the full weight of air attack. Over 250 planes from Task Force 38 mounted five separate attacks.

The *Yamato* and the *Nagato* were each damaged by two bomb hits but the *Musashi* bore the brunt. An estimated 13 torpedoes hit her on the port side and seven more on the starboard side, as well as 17 bombs and 18 near-misses. Even her massive protection could not stand up to such punishment and Kurita was forced to leave her behind. She finally sank about eight hours after the attacks had begun, but the fifth attack was the last. Kurita was not to know it, but Halsey had taken the bait and the whole of his Fast Carrier Task Force was in hot pursuit of Ozawa, leaving the invasion armada off Samar undefended. To the appalled Americans it was a nightmare come to life, the giant *Yamato* and her consorts attacking flimsy escort carriers and their destroyer escorts. Nor were the CVEs' aircraft armed with weapons for attacking battleships; their job was to provide support for the troops ashore, and no dive-bombers were embarked. And yet the impossible happened – the Japanese withdrew without achieving the destruction of the invasion fleet,

although they sank an escort carrier, two destroyers and a destroyer escort.

As predicted, Ozawa's force was devastated when Halsey's planes caught up with it off Cape Engano. All the carriers were sunk but the converted carrier-battleships *Hyuga* and *Ise* both escaped and made their way back to Japan. But the most devastating defeat of all had overtaken Nishimura when he entered Surigao Strait just after midnight on 24–25 October. His force, comprising two destroyers leading the flagship *Yamashiro*, the *Fuso* and the heavy cruiser *Mogami* in line ahead with two more destroyers guarding the flanks, brushed aside attacks by PT-Boats and was then attacked by destroyers, Nishimura appears to have taken no evasive action, and at 0207 a spread of probably five torpedoes hit the *Fuso* amidships. Oil fuel caught fire and then a series of explosions tore the ship in half, but instead of sinking the two burning halves drifted apart. Both Japanese and American lookouts reported two blazing ships, and the after section took an hour to sink.

Behind the destroyers and PT-Boats was waiting Admiral Jesse B Oldendorf's Battle Line, old battleships but equipped with the latest fire control and radar. At 0253 they opened fire at 22,800 yards, first the *Tennessee* and *West Virginia* and then the *Maryland* and the flagship *Mississippi*. Incredibly the *Yamashiro* seemed impervious to broadsides of 14-inch and 16-inch shells, and even torpedoes, but finally she slowed to a dead stop and lay blazing furiously in the water. No ship could take that sort of pounding indefinitely and at 0319 she finally rolled over and sank. Surigao Strait was a fitting swansong for the battleship, particularly as both the Japanese and the American ships were veterans of an earlier generation. They may have been overtaken by the carriers in importance but when it came down to a question of stopping a strong force of ships, just as the British had found with the *Bismarck* the battleship's guns were the final arbiter.

The Imperial Japanese Navy was all but wiped out at Leyte, for although aircraft remained there were no trained pilots to fly them and no carriers; there were still surface ships but no fuel to enable them to put to sea. As the remnants of the Air Force immolated themselves in *kamikaze* attacks on the invasion fleet around Okinawa the Navy planned the biggest suicide of all. The giant *Yamato* was ordered to use the remaining oil fuel (there was only enough for a one-way trip) for a last sortie against the invaders. Although there was talk of blasting her way through the ring of Allied ships and then beaching herself

on Okinawa as a huge gun-emplacement, the real purpose was to act as live bait. By drawing off as many carrier planes it was hoped to leave the air-space around Okinawa clear for a gigantic *kamikaze* attack on the transports. Code-named *Ten-Go*, the force comprized the *Yamato*, the light cruiser *Yahagi* and eight destroyers under the command of Vice-Admiral Ito.

At 1600 on 6 April 1945 the *Ten-Go* force slipped away from Tokuyama Bay and headed towards Okinawa in a ring formation with the *Yamato* in the centre. At 1220 the next day the *Yamato* signalled that she could see large numbers of aircraft 33,000 yards off her port bow. At 1232 she opened fire, using even the 18-inch guns to fire a 'splash barrage' against low-flying attackers. At 1240 the first bombs hit her and ten minutes later she was hit on the port side by torpedoes. After another eight torpedoes on the port side and two on the starboard side the flooding got out of control and the list could no longer be corrected. After the last torpedo hit at 1417 the giant ship was listing 20 degrees and the order 'abandon ship' was given. She finally capsized and erupted in a huge explosion, probably caused by internal fires reaching the magazines.

Although the fast carriers had dominated the Pacific War the battleship retained her prestige to the end. When General MacArthur and Admiral Nimitz witnessed the unconditional surrender of Japan it was on the quarterdeck of the USS *Missouri*, while HMS *Duke of York* was moored nearby representing the British Pacific Fleet.

Above: The US *Mississippi* during a bombardment operation.
Left: The quarterdeck of the USS Massachusetts (BB.59).
Below: The massive US invasion fleet off Leyte, October 1944.
The battleships *Colorado* and *Texas* are among the ships in the foreground.

THE END OF AN ERA?

The battleship was officially dead but she would not lie down. A surprising number remained in commission after the Second World War, mainly because their large hulls provided useful accommodation for sailors and cadets under training. Their spaciousness also made them ideal flagships.

The US Navy now had four of the magnificent *Iowas* in commission. All the old battleships were rapidly decommissioned and laid up for disposal, with the exception of the *Mississippi*, which was earmarked for conversion to a gunnery training and trials ship. Even the two *North Carolinas* and the four *South Dakotas* went into the 'mothball fleet' early in 1947.

The battleship might have remained in limbo, rather like a domesticated dinosaur, had it not been for the Korean War. When the North Korean Army crossed the 38th Parallel in 1950 the *Missouri* was the only US battleship in commission. In September that year she was sent to South Korea and served three tours of duty between 1950 and 1953. She was joined by her three sisters and they proved invaluable for shore bombardment. Again and again the battleships were able to give rapid and precise fire support to ground troops, their biggest advantage being their ability to 'loiter' and resume the bombardment if the enemy showed signs of further activity. No matter what weight of ordnance could be delivered by aircraft they always had to return to base after a short interval whereas the battleship could usually be called up to provide more gunfire.

The four *Iowas* remained active until 1955–58. In 1953 the *Iowa* and *Wisconsin* joined the last British battleship HMS *Vanguard* in the big NATO exercise 'Mariner' in the North Atlantic. All three showed off their enormous endurance by refuelling all the escorting destroyers in the task force. When the *Wisconsin* decommissioned on 8 March 1958 at Bayonne, New Jersey it seemed that end of the story had been reached, the first time since 1895 that the US Navy had no battleship in service. But soon the Vietnam War was absorbing an increasing American military effort and there was a vociferous demand from the US Marine Corps for something heavier than 8-inch gunfire support. Finally in 1967 permission was granted to bring a battleship forward from reserve.

The choice fell on the *New Jersey*, last in commission exactly a decade earlier. She was taken in hand at Philadelphia Navy Yard in August 1967 and recommissioned the following April. The *New Jersey*'s comeback was short but effective. On the 'gun line' in Vietnam she spent 120 days in all, of which 47 days were continuous. During the Second World War she had fired a total of 771 16-inch shells, during the Korean War she had fired nearly 7000 rounds, but this time she fired 5688 rounds and 15,000 rounds of 5-inch as well. Sadly she was taken out of commission in December 1969 but in 1981 her reactivation was again authorized. There is even talk of rearming her sisters with Cruise missiles to serve as flagships. The battleship is not yet finished.

Right: A Sea Knight helicopter lands on the *New Jersey* while the battleship is alongside the ammunition ship *Mount Katmai*, off Vietnam in July 1968.
Top left: The *New Jersey* and the carrier *Coral Sea* return to the US from Vietnam in April 1969.
Top right: The USS *Idaho* bombards Okinawa in 1945.

INDEX

Acknowledgments

The author would like to thank David Eldred, the designer, R. Watson who compiled the index and Richard Natkiel who prepared the maps. The following agencies supplied the illustrations:

Author's collection: p 55 (bottom)
Bibliothek für Zeitgeschichte, Stuttgart: pp 34–35
Bison picture library: p 27 (lower)
Charles E Brown: p 47 (center)
Bundesarchiv: pp 31 (top rt), 35 (top left), 39 (center)
Central Naval Museum, Leningrad, via Boris Lemarchko: p 26
Conway Picture Library: pp 48–49
ECPA: p 35 (top rt)
Foto Drüppel: pp 32–33, 55 (top)
Aldo Fraccaroli: pp 24–25
Imperial War Museum, London: pp 17 (top), 18, 18–19, 19 (top), 22–23, 33, 38–39, 39 (top left), 40–41, 42–43, 44–45, 48, 50–51
Humphrey Joel: p 45
Musée de la Marine: pp 10, 36–37
Museo Storico Navale, Venice: p 19 (center)
National Maritime Museum: pp 6–7 (two pics), 16, 17 (lower), 20, 30, 30–31, 31 (top left), 46–47
Maps © Richard Natkiel: pp 26, 27, 39, 42, 43, 51, 54, 59
US Navy: pp 10–11, 11 (bottom two), 12 (two pics), 13, 23, 28 (lower), 35 (center), 46, 47 (top), 57 (two pics), 58, 58–59, 60, 61, 62–63